My Father's
Guru

Also by Jeffrey Moussaieff Masson

DOGS NEVER LIE ABOUT LOVE:
Reflections on the Emotional World of Dogs

WHEN ELEPHANTS WEEP:
The Emotional Lives of Animals

FINAL ANALYSIS*:
The Making and Unmaking of a Psychoanalyst

AGAINST THERAPY:
Emotional Tyranny and the Myth of Psychological Healing

A DARK SCIENCE:
Women, Sexuality and Psychiatry in the Nineteenth Century

THE ASSAULT ON TRUTH*:
Freud's Suppression of the Seduction Theory

THE OCEANIC FEELING:
The Origins of Religious Sentiment in Ancient India

THE COMPLETE LETTERS OF SIGMUND FREUD
TO WILHELM FLIESS 1887–1904
(Editor)

THE PEACOCK'S EGG: Love Poems from Ancient India
(Translations by W. S. Merwin, Editor)

* Published by POCKET BOOKS

For orders other than by individual consumers, Pocket Books grants a discount on the purchase of **10 or more** copies of single titles for special markets or premium use. For further details, please write to the Vice-President of Special Markets, Pocket Books, 1633 Broadway, New York, NY 10019-6785, 8th Floor.

For information on how individual consumers can place orders, please write to Mail Order Department, Simon & Schuster Inc., 200 Old Tappan Road, Old Tappan, NJ 07675.

Jeffrey Moussaieff Masson

My Father's Guru

A JOURNEY THROUGH SPIRITUALITY AND DISILLUSION

For Elaine & Arnold from Jeff & Leila in memory of a wonderful dinner

POCKET BOOKS

New York   London   Toronto   Sydney   Tokyo   Singapore

POCKET BOOKS, a division of Simon & Schuster Inc.
1230 Avenue of the Americas, New York, NY 10020

ISBN: 0-671-02573-2

First Pocket Books trade paperback printing October 1998

10 9 8 7 6 5 4 3 2 1

Cover design by Tom McKeveny, courtesy of the author

Printed in the U.S.A.

To the memory of my father

Contents

Introduction

On Venus There Are No Cars

"P.B., why is it that you don't drive a car?" I asked Paul Brunton, my father's guru.

He smiled, somewhat mysteriously, and waited for a rather long time before answering. The smile conveyed to me that he was remembering times long past, that there were things he could not *yet* tell me, that I was naïve yet endearing, that there was a bond between us. Children invest a great deal in certain adults. For me, he was one of those adults. I was perhaps ten, he was about fifty.

"Jeffrey, on Venus there are no cars."

I waited for more of an explanation, but he looked off into a vast distance, and I knew that no further answer would be forthcoming. And how could I ask for more? Had he not just hinted—forget hinting, he had as much as said that he came from Venus. P.B. was from Venus! What unfathomable good fortune had brought him here to Earth, to this very house on Park Oak Drive in the Hollywood Hills, where I lived with my parents, Jacques and Diana Masson, and my sister Linda to bless us with his presence, delight us with his teachings, elevate us to realms of spiritual enlightenment that would otherwise remain completely beyond our reach?

This is a book about me and Paul Brunton, my father's guru, a man with human failings. It is also about my father and mother and sister and uncle, but primarily it is about my own relationship to P.B. and to Indian spirituality while I was growing up.

Who was P.B.? Paul Brunton was an English author of books about mysticism. He was born in London on October 21, 1898, and died in Vevey, Switzerland, on July 27, 1981, at the age of eighty-two. His first book, published in 1934, was entitled *A Search in Secret India* and tells the story of his travels in India looking for mystics, yogis, and seers. It was one of the first and perhaps the most popular book introducing Indian mysticism to the West. During his life he published eleven books, the last of which, in 1952, was *The Spiritual Crisis of Man*.

Paul Brunton was my father's guru. He lived for many years with our family. We called him, as did most of his other friends, P.B. He was inordinately short, just over five feet tall, and very frail, weighing only slightly more than a hundred pounds. He spoke in low, measured tones with a pronounced English accent. His face seemed always in repose, and he had a far-off look. He cultivated the calm, inward-looking gaze of the sage. Much of my childhood was spent in his presence.

In none of his books did he reveal anything at all about his personal life. Evidently he was born with the name Raphael Hurst, and took, first Brunton Paul, then Paul Brunton as a pen name. Although little is known of his early life, in fact little is known of his later life either. This was by his choice. He insisted on secrecy and mystery. Indeed, if I can think of a single word that is most appropriate to Paul Brunton, his life, his writings, his interests, it would be *secret*. He liked the word and everything it stood for.

It is possible that the reason for this has to do with secrets in his own life—that is, facts he did not want others to know about. I am not sure, because these facts have never entirely emerged, though little bits dribble out. He was, for example, half Jewish; he hid this fact. He had cosmetic surgery performed on his nose and encouraged some of his Jewish disciples (including my parents) to do the same. He claimed that his first wife was a hermaphrodite, though I have no idea what he meant by this. Perhaps he was joking. He married a second time, a third, and a fourth. His third and fourth wife was the same person, Evangeline Young, who venerates P.B. to this day as her guru. But he never mentioned his marriages in any of his books. After his death, his only child, a son named Kenneth Hurst, born to his second wife, wrote a biography of his father in 1988. This biography reveals little about the man himself. His son became his "disciple" and the biography is an adoring hagiography.

Most of the books that Paul Brunton wrote were immensely successful. There were a series of them in quick succession: After his first book, *A Search in Secret India*, came the small and very popular *The Secret Path*, in 1935, followed the same year by *A Search in Secret Egypt*, which evidently rivaled in popularity the first book; *A Message from Arunachala* came out in 1936, followed by *A Hermit in the Himalayas* in 1937. All of these early books went into many printings, as did some of the later ones. *The Quest of the Overself* appeared in 1938, and in 1939 came *Discover Yourself*. *The Hidden Teaching Beyond Yoga* came out in 1941, followed by *The Wisdom of the Overself* in 1942. The tiny (forty-five pages) *Indian Philosophy and Modern Culture*, P.B.'s "thesis," was published a few years later. After *The Spiritual Crisis of Man* was published in 1952, he published no more books during the rest of his life, but he continued to make notes and "do research" about mysticism, especially Indian mysticism. The results were published after his death, in the sixteen volumes of *The Notebooks of Paul Brunton*, all of which are currently still in print. Many of his earlier books are also in print, and there has been something of a renewed interest in his philosophy. The Paul Brunton Philosophical Foundation in New York State is dedicated to propagating his books and teachings.

Attracted by his writings, a number of people in Europe, Asia, and the United States corresponded with Paul Brunton, and many of them came to visit him. Some were accepted as "disciples," though there is some question how many. My father's older brother, Bernard, was one of these. My uncle Bernard wrote to P.B. after reading his first book and asked to become his disciple. He stayed in his orbit for the next twenty-five years. One of his first acts was to inform his younger brother, my father, that he had found a guru for both of them. My father wrote P.B. and right after the war went to India to be with him.

My father was first hooked in through a "vision" of P.B.'s that showed my father at forty having developed "occult powers" and entering into "spiritual consciousness." And so my father waited impatiently to become forty, and when he complained, at forty-one, that he was still unaware of any occult powers, P.B. reminded him that in the vision he was *some* forty years of age, which could be broadly interpreted. By fifty, my father had more or less given up hope, though he never entirely abdicated his long and increasingly hopeless and lonely vigil.

Paul Brunton never owned a home. He stayed instead with various students of his writings, among whom my father and mother figured prominently. His financial situation was always unclear. Presumably he made a modest living from his books, some of which were widely translated into European languages and went into multiple editions. He did not seem to have many possessions. He positively shunned the limelight and almost never made public appearances of any kind. He appears to have had no higher education, though he used the title "Doctor" and claimed to have had a Ph.D. bestowed upon him by an unnamed university in the United States in recognition of his contribution to Oriental studies. He lived for many years in India, then divided his time between the United States and Europe. When he was in Europe, he traveled constantly from one country to another, though the purpose of these trips was never made clear.

By the time I was ten, I knew that P.B. was uniquely important to my parents, to a band of devoted "disciples," and especially to my father. He was a living "master," I was told, a man of spiritual substance who had been reincarnated on earth to help other less fortunate mortals—namely my family, his primary disciples, as I thought we were at the time. Actually, he was a great deal more promiscuous in his affections, practicing a kind of spiritual bigamy, since while presenting his relation to us as unique, he was a resident or quasi-resident guru of several families.

By the time I was twelve, my information began to grow. I found out that in the 1930s he had almost single-handedly introduced Indian mysticism to the West, through the teachings of Ramanamaharshi, a South Indian teacher whom he had visited in India. Pictures of this Indian sage were everywhere in our house. In a number of these photographs his gaze exhibits a look of astonished innocence and great purity. I was told as a child that, wherever I went, his large dark eyes would follow me. They did, and I experimented with other photos and discovered that the eyes in each did the same thing.

I tried to read P.B.'s books when I was younger but found them impenetrable. By the age of thirteen, they were my constant companions, providing fantasies of far-off places and mysterious mystic powers. At P.B.'s recommendation, I learned to chant Sanskrit verses, for which I found I had a surprising talent—surprising because I am more or less tone deaf. I was convinced I was "on the Path." I remember walking along the beach in Kailua, on the island of Oahu, when I was fourteen. My sister, eleven at the time, approached me with a "mundane" question, and I waved her away self-importantly: "Woman, I have just been reading *The Mysterious Kundalini* and cannot be disturbed in my contemplations." To her credit, Linda muttered, "What bullshit," and wandered off to a more companionable playmate. It was a mythological world filled with remote Tibetan monasteries, secret manuscripts, Indian masters with strange powers, and dark forces aligned against the forces of light. P.B. was a general in that spiritual army, and I was his young but valiant aide-de-camp.

I grew up in the shadow of a man who laid claim to enormous power, although not worldly power. It was quickly made clear to me that his power did not reside in the things of this earth. He did not have the external signs of power; he had little money, no home, few possessions. But wherever he went there were mysterious phone calls, hints in his conversations of immensely important meetings that nobody else was permitted to witness, hastily jotted notes, letters from odd places. All of this led us to believe that P.B. was conducting a secret counterwar, a spiritual campaign of such staggering significance that only the great mythological battles of ancient times could provide an analogy. P.B. was sometimes covertly and sometimes overtly offering our family a role in a vast and important "plan." The plan had to be kept secret. Enemies were lurking. The forces of evil were listening, waiting for their chance to infiltrate the headquarters of the forces of good. All of the people whom P.B. had chosen, or might choose, as his disciples were singularly favored. They were to be at the center of the salvation of the universe. There could be no greater honor. This was a universe as simply organized as a boy's adventure story. I found a similar atmosphere when I read Tolkien's *Lord of the Rings* years later.

Nobody desires a traumatic environment of any kind, and no child should have to endure one. There is, nonetheless, some satisfaction in discovering, however belatedly, that one has been subjected to such an environment. It helps to explain otherwise puzzling events.

When I went to university, I studied Sanskrit because I had grown up in a household in which this ancient Indian language was considered sacred. In abandoning my professorship in Sanskrit— psychologically at first, but literally later on—for psychoanalytic training, I thought I was leaving behind my spiritual past and freely choosing my own career, one unrelated to my childhood. But in my subsequent analytic career, I idealized Freud much as I had idealized P.B. and Indian philosophy. I remade my own analyst in the image of P.B.—pretty standard psychoanalytic stuff, but my analyst never even seemed to notice. He may have been too eager to play guru to want to disillusion me.

I did not find it the least strange (although others did) that I soon felt entitled to approach the formidable Kurt Eissler, doyen of the Freudian world in New York, while I was still a young analyst-in-training. He, too, was like a guru; I desperately wanted to be his spiritual son. Again, I was reenacting my earlier drama with P.B., only on a slightly larger scale. It was inevitable that I would seek to reproduce something of the excitement of my earlier life on this intellectual plane, and perhaps it will appear to others as inevitable that I should turn against my gurus, that I was "destined" to become a debunker.

I am, I finally realize, unusually sensitive to pretense, fraudulence, and lack of truthfulness. Growing up with a guru provided me with an opportunity to understand the guru/disciple phenomenon in its various manifestations and permutations. It may seem that I was still unmasking revenants of P.B. But learning the source of an interest, a preoccupation even, does not automatically invalidate the results of the inquiry. If people wear masks, unmasking seems to me a legitimate activity.

I wish to make it clear that P.B. was certainly no Jim Jones, not even a Bhaktivedanta, the guru of the Hare Krishnas, no Paramahansa Yogananda of the Self-Realization Fellowship, no Rajneesh from Poona or Oregon, no Maharshimaheshyogi, no Muktananda. He is not an egregious example of a false prophet. The story I have to tell about him is not an exposé in the classic sense, although I have nothing against such exposés. Tales by insiders of what really goes on in these cults are not only fascinating gossip, they are instructive of the kind of world this spirituality builds. But P.B. did not have the usual faults of overweening arrogance, sexual predation, murderous activities, ruthless greed, and insatiable appetite for luxury so often found among gurus. A guru cannot exist alone: To be a guru, it is necessary to have disciples. I was able to observe, especially in me and my father and in Paul Brunton, the clash, the romanticism, and the ultimate tragedy of these attempts to escape the imperfections of the human condition. I was a direct participant, and I did not escape its consequences.

For my sources in writing this book, I have used several hundred letters from P.B. to myself, my father, and my mother, and from us to him. My father has made available to me his diary written in India in 1945, when he first met P.B. I also have several hundred letters between my uncle Bernard and P.B. I have tape recordings of memories of P.B. from my mother, my father, my sister, and my uncle. I have also used P.B.'s published writings, as well as the sixteen volumes of *The Notebooks of Paul Brunton* published after his death.

Most of all, however, I have relied on my memory. I have reconstructed conversations based on memory and these other sources because I had no other choice.

I wish that I had access to tape recordings of the original conversations, or that I possessed the kind of memory that would enable me to remember verbatim things said to me forty years ago. I cannot claim that these are verbatim quotations. On the other hand, anyone who knew P.B. or who reads his books today (readily available in "metaphysical" bookstores and in libraries) will recognize P.B. in them. I have not ascribed to him any opinion for which there is not some external verification. I have not speculated, except when I explicitly say so. These reconstructions are not fictional; they are an attempt to be as accurate and authentic as possible. P.B. did not say or write things memorably. But for an eleven-year-old boy to be told by his father's guru, "My real home is the star Sirius, and when I die I will return there," the *content* of the statement was so astonishing as to be unforgettable. My memory recorded this exactly, with one discrepancy: I actually remember P.B. saying "Venus." But in his posthumously published writings, Sirius is used in a similar context, and I assume I merely remembered incorrectly. What impressed me as a child was not the name of the star or planet, but the fact that P.B. was saying he came from another planet. Similarly, I can remember sitting in our garden on the beach in Kailua in Hawaii, late in the evening with my sister Linda staring up at the illuminated sky. P.B. approached us and warned:

"Children, don't look at the moon. Look at Venus instead."

"Why?" we both wanted to know.

"Dark forces are on the moon."

"And Venus?" we asked eagerly.

"That is where the higher powers are."

This I cannot forget.

My editor at Addison-Wesley, Nancy Miller, has once again stood by me for each step of this book. She is the editor every writer hopes to have, and I am lucky beyond telling. I am honored and touched that Catharine MacKinnon took time away from her own important work to sit down and read this manuscript word for word, with a focus and concentration only she can bring to a serious topic. I am grateful to my uncle Bernard Masson (and his son Charles) for making his many letters to and from P.B. available to me and for telling me his memories of a thirty-some-year relationship. My sister, Linda Juson, and my mother, Diana Masson, did the same. But I am most of all grateful to my father, Jacques Victor Masson, for his many honest and painful conversations about P.B., the last of which we held today, his eightieth birthday. It is to my father that I dedicate this book.

Half Moon Bay, California
May 27, 1992

My Father's Guru

Chapter One

My Father and His Guru

I arrived in Mysore City, State of Mysore, South India, on Saturday, Decem-
ber 8th, 1945, at 8:40 P.M. and was met at the station by P.B. He immediately
said to me: "You are here for a certain purpose which will be revealed to you
before you leave. I wanted you to come here, that is why your trip was made
so easy."

So begins my father's diary of his four-month stay in South India, where he went to meet, for the first time, his guru, Paul Brunton.

My father was born Jacques Victor Masson in Paris in 1912. During his early childhood his family moved about a great deal, living in New York, Paris, and Jerusalem, where most of his family still live. He was always considered different and felt different from other members of his family: They were physically large where he was small; they were crude where he was sensitive; they were loud while he was quiet; they (especially his father) were violent while he was gentle. "He looks so refined," people would say when he was young. And who was he? Was he French because he was born in France? Or was he American because they moved to New York when he was small? Or Bukharan, because both his parents were from

Bukhara? Or Israeli, because that is where most of his family lived? He was not even certain what his language was: French? Bukharan? English? Hebrew? Did he live with his mother? His father? His uncle? He moved with each in turn, unsure to whom he belonged. He lived in Paris until he was two, but when World War I broke out, his mother and three sisters went to New York, where his father was living, and stayed in New York for five years. The family then moved back to Paris, and in 1920, when my father was eight, he moved in with his father's older brother, Sam, and his wife, Ida. In 1926, when he was fourteen, he moved to Jerusalem and lived in the Bukharan quarter with his father and his three sisters (Henriette, Vicki, and Rachel), surrounded by relatives. He remained there until 1930, when he was eighteen.

At that time his father was in his forties and had remarried a beautiful Bukharan Jewish woman, who was only eighteen, the same age as his son. She knew he had been previously married but had no idea that he had five living children. My grandfather was in Shanghai, China, and asked my father to bring his new bride and join him there. Shortly after arriving, however, his father and new stepmother left for an extended business trip to Bombay, Peshawar, and Burma, and my father was left alone with no money. He spoke French and Hebrew but almost no English and no Chinese. He was eighteen but looked fifteen. He felt completely abandoned. His father sent him several hundred kilos of rough lapis lazuli, which was almost unsalable in those days of economic depression. After about a year he managed to sell some of it. During the 1931–32 Japanese invasion, he joined the Shanghai Volunteer Corps.

At twenty, my father decided to migrate to the United States. In 1932, he left Shanghai on the SS *Hoover* to San Francisco, arriving in the middle of the Great Depression. He survived by doing odd jobs and working in a linen store on Hollywood Boulevard. In 1936 his employer, Norman Jemal, sent him to Honolulu, Hawaii, to open two stores. A year later he began his own linen business in Denver, Colorado. He moved his business to Tucson, Arizona, that same year and then in 1938 to Detroit, obeying a restlessness that has never left him.

My grandfather had not had any contact with my father in eight years. One day in 1938 out of the blue he called: "Jacques, come to Chicago. I have a prospective bride for you." In Chicago, my father met his father at Zion's Kosher Restaurant on Roosevelt Road. The owners were my grandmother and grandfather. The woman who was to become my mother, Diana Zeiger, joined the two men at the table, and within five months, on January 22, 1939, she and my father were married in Chicago. The next year my father opened a large linen store on Michigan Avenue and another on South State Street, an enormous five-story store devoted exclusively to linen. At that time, it was one of the largest in the world. Two years later I was born, on March 28, 1941, at the Chicago Osteopathic Hospital; even then my parents were interested in alternative medicine. A year later, my parents moved to Los Angeles, California, where my father began a new career as a wholesale dealer in precious stones and pearls, the business in which most of his family had been engaged for as long as anyone could remember. He was successful almost immediately and has continued this business to this day.

During the war, my father was drafted but could not pass the medical test due to kidney problems. He nonetheless attempted to enlist in the Intelligence Division of the U.S. Army, since he spoke fluent French, but he was rejected for lack of qualifications. Although my parents were Jewish, they had no sense of the tragedy taking place in Europe and did not know what had happened until many years later. They were completely engrossed in a different world, the world of mysticism.

My father first learned of P.B. from his older brother, Bernard. The appeal of P.B. to Bernard is impossible to understand without knowing something more of the family history.

My great-grandfather, Shlomo Moussaieff, was born in Bukhara, a city along the silk route in the Central Asian province of Uzbekistan (formerly part of the South West Soviet Union in Asia). He was a gem merchant from a Jewish family with a strong interest in Jewish mysticism (Kabbala), a system of esoteric Theosophy with occult elements developed by rabbis during the twelfth and thirteenth centuries. He had five sons and two daughters. One of the sons was my grandfather, Rafael Haim (later known as Henri), born in Bukhara on July 23, 1883. He, too, was interested in Jewish mysticism and became a gem merchant. At nineteen he married Penina (Hebrew for "pearl") Abdul Kerjan, a young, pretty Bukharan Jewish girl. They moved to Palestine, where my uncle Bernard, their first child, was born in 1905. In 1910 the family moved to Paris, where my father, Jacques (Jack) Victor was born on May 27, 1912.

My grandfather was a large, passionate man, colorful and given to unconventional ways. In France he was a pearl and diamond merchant and led a flamboyant life. I was told that he seduced every girl and woman around him whether they were eight or fifty-eight. Nor did he exempt his own family. His wife came from a very simple background. When she arrived in France, she spoke no French and knew nobody. She sat on the floor in the middle of the apartment and attempted to cook rice pilaf in the ways she had learned as a child. She ate with her hands, which embarrassed my more worldly grandfather, who started dating and sleeping with dancers from the Folies Bergères. The five children came in quick succession, and my grandfather got fed up with both his wife and the children and decided to move out, leaving my grandmother with no means of livelihood. She still spoke no French, had no profession, and knew nobody outside her immediate family. She had no money to run the household, nothing even to feed the children. Rumor has it (I heard this from my father's cousin, Shlomo Haim Moussaieff, who now lives in London as a hugely successful gem merchant) that my grandfather ordered one of his employees in Paris, a man called Nissim Valero (who was eventually to become an Israeli judge), to seduce his wife, so that he could accuse her of infidelity. My grandfather was later to claim that my father, Jacques, was the son of this Valero, though my father laughs at the idea and says it is patently untrue, and his father knew it. It was his idea of a cruel joke.

One day in 1920 in Paris, my grandmother Penina decided that she could stand her life no more. She went to the Diamond Exchange on the rue Cadet and sent her son Bernard, not yet fifteen at the time, inside to call his father. He refused to see her. She insisted that she had something of great importance to tell him. Finally, he came to the top of the stairs and asked her what she wanted. She told him in Bukharan that she had no food to feed the children and they were all starving. He told her: "Go to hell," and turned to leave, when Penina started shrieking at him with cries of rage and curses in Bukharan. She then pulled a gun from her skirt and shot five times at my grandfather. He gave a loud yell and made a leap at his wife. Bernard swiped at his father's legs and floored him. One bullet grazed my grandfather's eye and left him bleeding profusely, but he was not seriously injured. Pandemonium broke out, with my grandfather shouting over and over, "My own son came to kill me!" The police were summoned, and my grandmother was put in jail. Bernard did not see her for nine years. The children then went to Lycée Michelet, a boarding school. Eventually my father went to live with a brother of his father, Uncle Sam, and Bernard moved to Palestine. Penina moved to New York, where she died of Bright's disease in 1931. She had six children, not a single one of whom was with her when she died.

In Palestine, Bernard lived with his grandfather, Shlomo (a popular name in our family) Moussaieff, a wealthy gem merchant who had an all-absorbing interest in Jewish mysticism, Kabbala. He had an immense library, and Bernard spent a great deal of time reading Hebrew books about the Kabbala. Bernard was particularly captivated, as any adolescent might have been, with the notion that certain people have powers, mysterious powers, that exert an influence on the real world. These powers exist in all traditions, whether they are called miracles, or yogic powers, or gifts. They include such things as being able to tell the future, to read another person's mind, to move an object without touching it, to levitate, to become invisible, and so on. I said "any adolescent," but I think I mean especially one whose life is filled with trauma and unhappiness, as Bernard's was. To imagine that there is a world totally different from the one you are living in, a world of benign magicians of immense power, is bound to comfort anybody at the mercy of bigger, stronger, and meaner people.

Eventually Bernard left Palestine, moved to the United States, and entered the U.S. Navy. By 1934, at twenty-nine, he was chief petty officer in the navy yard in Charleston, South Carolina. It was there, on February 23, 1938, that he made his first attempt to connect with P.B.:

Navy Yard

Charleston, S.C.
23 February 1938

E. P. Dutton & Co. Inc.
300 Fourth Avenue,
New York, N.Y.

Dear Sirs:

I desire to communicate with Mr. Paul Brunton, the author of *The Secret Path, Search in Secret India*, etc.

I would appreciate it very much if you would kindly inform me as to how to address myself in order to contact the gentleman by letter.

The letter was signed B. A. Grand. Bernard regarded "Grand" as a kind of *nom de guerre* to which he was entitled in order to hide the fact that he was Jewish. It may be, too, that he rather liked the elevated sound of it. In any event, this letter began a thirty-year correspondence and acquaintance on the part of my uncle Bernard with the author Paul Brunton.

My father first heard about Paul Brunton from Bernard in 1939, when Bernard was thirty-four years old, and my father was twenty-seven. My father looked up to his older brother. He regarded Bernard as a kind of genius plagued with bad luck. Bernard gave my father three of the first books P.B. wrote, *A Search in Secret India, A Message from Arunachala*, and *A Hermit in the Himalayas*, and he spoke to him at length about mysticism and yoga but especially about magic powers, some-

thing Bernard had been interested in ever since he studied the Kabbala with his grandfather in Jerusalem. He told Jacques that P.B.
had told him that "the only reason we are born in this world is to
attain Self Realization." I was to hear these words many times in my
childhood: "Is he self-realized?" was commonly asked. "I was convinced that Bernard was telling the truth," my father told me recently,
and he decided then and there that he wished to become a "disciple"
of this great man.

He wrote his first letter to P.B. in 1940, asking for spiritual
assistance. P.B. wrote back, and so began their correspondence.

P.B. was in India throughout the Second World War, living there
as a guest of the Maharaja of Mysore. At the end of the war, my father
decided to travel to Mysore to visit P.B. The time was not propitious
for travel. It was 1945. I was four years old, and was being raised as if I
were the incarnation of a great Indian yogi. My father was determined that he would visit India and see these yogis for himself. The
war having ended only a few months before, transportation was
extremely difficult to obtain, especially for civilians, but somehow he
managed to convince the U.S. Army's Air Transport Command to
take him to Bombay.

My father arrived in Mysore in early December and the next
evening wrote my mother a letter:

Modern Cafe. Dasa Prakash. Mysore City. Sunday, December 9th, 1945.
Dearest Angel:

I arrived here yesterday at 8:30 P.M. and was met at the station by
P.B. himself. It was dark and there were a lot of passengers—but
he greeted me instantly. We then went to the Hotel. After I
registered we went for a long walk, then to his house which is a
Villa opposite the Maharajah's palace. Then for another long
walk and back to the Hotel. I am making notes of what he tells
me, and shall show them to you one day. Will keep a full diary. I
will learn a lot here dearest and it is very very fortunate that I
came. He told me he did not want any one to come but me. Not
M [a Chicago lawyer] who wanted to come three months ago,

or Bernard. He told them he did not wish to see them. So you see how fortunate I am. He said I had a certain thing to learn and later on I would understand the reason I had to come to India instead of waiting a few months to see him in the States. Anyway he will be tremendously busy when he goes back there. Here there is no one else to interfere. Please do not show this to anyone. . . . Today, Sunday, he came to visit me in the Hotel and told me that we shall start my spiritual work today, also that he will give me some books on meditation for me to study. He will pick me up after lunch. . . . Mysore City is a very beautiful place to live in, much nicer than Palm Springs; it is very quiet and peaceful, there are large parks and the Maharajah of Mysore's Palace is just like a 1001 nights dream. His Highness the Maharajah of Mysore is a very modern man and his state is the finest in all India, it is very progressive and constructive. God bless him. It is known as the "Garden City of India." If you came here you would love it very much. The climate is ideal. . . . How lucky I was to come by plane! I am one of the few if not the only civilians who came here not on urgent business by plane. Destiny has indeed been very good to me. . . . Monday morning— Dec. 10, 1945. After lunch P.B. and I went for a long walk on the palace grounds; I took some color pictures of a Dome with a real gold top. Saw the Palace garage which houses about 40 high priced cars. Dussberg, Rolls Royce, and others. Then went to P.B.'s house [Jasmine Villa, Hyderali Road], had a long talk, read a while. Had tea with him and later on went for a long walk to the Zoo—had long discussions about various topics. You don't know how fortunate I am, it's just like taking a three year university course in 3 weeks. He has a very good sense of humor and we had some hearty laughs. The late Maharajah of Mysore was one of his best friends; kept P.B.'s picture on his desk constantly, gave him a big Dussberg car with a chauffeur and a big Palace to live in. Among P.B.'s students were a lot of high Ministers in Egypt who later rose to very high positions in the government—After our long walk we rested then we meditated. Spoke to P.B. about you dearest and he told me if you could not meditate then you should pray every day, praying should be easy for you dearest, just pour your heart out and pray daily. I will help you meditate and go on the path when I return. After meditating we walked to my hotel and I asked P.B. if he cared to have dinner with me; he said he would not mind celebrating our first day together, so we had a nice vegetarian meal, then talked and he went home—One feels at ease in his company, he is very friendly and frank. It's a very wonderful thing for me to be here.

Why was my father there? What did he believe? Almost everything my father knew about Paul Brunton before he met him he had heard from his brother Bernard. Bernard, my father later told me, "had completely brainwashed me. He told me P.B. was an avatar, that is, an incarnation of the godhead, that he was an 'adept' with tremendous occult powers. I was completely certain it was true. It was only due to my good karma that I was going to meet this extraordinary being." He believed that P.B. did indeed have extraordinary powers. P.B. did little to disenchant him.

Rivalry among disciples is endemic to cults and cultlike associations, and this one was no exception. Bernard had told my father in 1940 that he, Bernard, was my father's guru, and my father had more or less accepted this. Now here he was with a *real* guru, with Bernard back in the United States. It was a major triumph.

P.B. told my father, as he did Bernard and all others who came to him, that "discipleship under an adept is a privilege which can never be bought." The only way it could be earned was over vast stretches of time, which was why more than one incarnation was required. It was all a matter of karma. Destiny had brought my father to P.B.; it was not to be ascribed to his own puny will. And destiny is very choosy. "The adept," P.B. said, "does not seek to recruit disciples. He knows that the few who could absorb his help will come by destiny."

All of the disciples were made to feel that they were chosen, that they were special, unique, and extremely privileged. "It is divinely ordained," explained P.B. P.B. let it be known that he accepted very few disciples. He would not teach the masses; he would not help them: "Ordinary aspirants are left to the guidance of more advanced disciples." The master simply could not waste his time on them. Only those who had prepared themselves with "self-purification, mystical methods and philosophic understanding" could hope to come into the presence of the master. Actually, it is doubtful that P.B. was ever given an opportunity to teach the masses. It is unlikely that thousands were clamoring to hear him, or that he received many letters expressing the desire to become his disciples. But it would have risked his dignity to acknowledge this, perhaps. So my father and others, like my uncle Bernard, were given to understand that innumerable people desperately wanted to become P.B.'s disciples.

P.B. told my father that he had tested his disciples in former lives, and he would test them again now. Each day there would be a test. There had to be a "probationary novitiate before acceptance as a regular full-fledged student, with access to his intimate circle" could be realized. True, P.B. explained to my father, he corresponded with hundreds of people and granted interviews rather freely, but "I personally instruct or train very few." Jack was delighted with his luck.

As for the tests, the major one seemed to be to make life for the disciple unpleasant, to ask him to do tasks for the guru that appeared unreasonable, silly, or a waste of time. The disciple had to be willing to make these sacrifices without hesitation and with a smile. My father and his brother were to be tested on many occasions. For the moment, P.B. said, it was time to be practical. P.B. was not unmindful of or ungrateful for my father's ability to make money. P.B. wanted his disciples to bond with each other around their guru. And so he deplored the rivalry between Jack and his brother and told him, "If two brothers, both on the same spiritual path, cannot get along with each other, how can we expect nations to live in peaceful coexistence?" It was a fair point, and yet P.B. did much to fan the rivalry between them and would continue to do so for the next twenty years.

Within minutes of meeting him, P.B. was boasting to my father of his position, his knowledge, his past. But the boasts sounded to my father like simple declarations of fact—information he had to have.

The late king venerated him, P.B. said, and forced tokens of gratitude (a car, a small palace) upon him. I don't know how much of this was true. There is an old tradition in India in which a king handsomely rewards somebody with spiritual power. It is almost a superstition. The late maharaja may have felt that P.B. was possibly such a person and that it was best to play it safe. It is also possible that P.B. imagined it. At the time of my father's first meeting, in any event, P.B. had no car and no chauffeur, and his modest bungalow was anything but a small palace. There are no other eyewitnesses, and as far as I know, nobody ever wrote about this except P.B. himself. Actually, P.B. only hinted at it in his writings and told people like my father about it verbally. My father was prepared to believe it all. He was, he says now, very gullible.

My father clearly believed he was being singled out—and indeed he was. The traditional dance of master and disciple had begun. Jack felt himself elevated and special in the presence of this special and elevated man. Only if P.B. was an adept with occult powers could my father maintain his special status, so it was important that he have these qualities. If P.B. was such a being, then their meeting could not be accidental, just one of those things that happen in life; it had to have been planned, it had to have been destined. The hand of destiny was axiomatic. P.B. needed my father as much as my father needed him. What is a master without a disciple? P.B. depended upon the constant reassurance that a fawning acolyte could give. This subservient manner was a constant reminder of the stature of the guru. I can remember when I was teaching Sanskrit at the University of Toronto, my greatest fear was that the next day no students would show up. "Why should we?" they would say. "We aren't learning anything worthwhile." I needed them to reappear to validate what I was doing. No doubt P.B. too liked to see my father reappear, grateful for whatever he had imagined he received. No doubt they did give each other something, though perhaps not what they thought. A genuine friendship was forming, even if its premises were false, or other than what they seemed.

Certainly my father wanted something no person could ever give him, and P.B. claimed to be able to give my father what no person can ever give another. One wanted, the other offered, transcendence of this world, spiritual enlightenment, and wisdom. Such yearnings and such offers are clearly evident in the actual diary that my father started writing the same day he wrote my mother:

> P.B. told me: I eat very simple food and live almost like a monk. Yes, he had met [me] in a previous life. You see, once a guru is born he is usually born with all his former disciples and no matter in what part of the world they are, they are bound to get together sooner or later. Sometimes it takes 20 years to meet. Once the Chela meets his guru a certain contact is formed and another meeting is not necessary. A telepathic cord is formed, and the presence of the guru can be mentally formed. . . . I have accepted only one student—he is an Indian, he obtained illumination, he is the only one I accepted as a student.

P.B. was already forging the notion of a secret brotherhood. All of P.B.'s disciples had been together in a former life and were destined to meet again in this life, to take up once again the search. It was a compelling idea. How nice to think that encounters are not random, chance, but that there is some all-seeing benevolent eye that is watching out for our good, busily bringing people together who should be together or who already were together. Especially if you meet somebody and there is an immediate spark, it is attractive to imagine that the encounter repeats an earlier relationship. Life might be more interesting or more meaningful if this were true (like survivors, we could seek out our real friends). My father's trip to Mysore would have had purpose and not be just a futile search based on a casual misunderstanding. Both my father and P.B. were determined to believe this was true and to act accordingly. It definitely was a form of intimacy, even if based, as I believe it was, on false premises. The intimacy itself was real, beyond whatever false idea made it possible.

At their first meeting, P.B. gave my father a secret mantra: "You are the first student I have ever given a mantra to." My father was delighted. "Before you leave, you may get a glimpse of the Light. I will try to give it to you. Make yourself receptive and still your thoughts." They meditated. "At nine P.M. for a second the lights went out. P.B.'s body was luminous, full of light." P.B. believed it was his function, and that he had the ability, to "awaken people to the divine presence within themselves." He did this, however, he later said, "mysteriously by some unknown process." Unknown, that is, to the disciple. P.B. often said that "when the first meeting with the destined master takes place, the seeker will experience an emotion such as he has had with no other person before. The inner attraction will be immense, the feeling of fated gravity intense." This is precisely what my father felt, much like falling in love.

That day P.B. also gave my father a ring of a snake eating its own tail, which he still has today. He said it had belonged to Allāh Bahā', the founder of the Baha'i faith. He told him: "Keep this ring and whenever you look at it think that you are here in this world to obtain spiritual consciousness. You can change the color according to your mood, by reversing the top of the ring." When my father attempted to change the color, he was unsuccessful, but he attributed his failure to his own character flaws: "I must try harder."

The "training" began immediately. Instruction was passed on silently during meditation. It was during meditation that P.B. was able, like a skilled clinician, to make his diagnosis. On December 11, they meditated together, and P.B. told my father (as he wrote that evening in his diary), "You are still surrounded by gross matter which I will have to break through, it comes from your former associations. Now once it is broken it will not surround you any more. Yes, once you attain that 'PEACE' it remains with you. You feel it first with every meditation, then all the time, even when you are very active. You shall have that Peace and it will remain with you; then every time you meditate it will be a tremendous source of joy to you, and it shall always remain with you. Next time we meditate I shall 'do' something to you." P.B. claimed that he could grant an illumination to others, if he wished, and they were "karmically" ready (though the two seem contradictory) by merely touching them with the tip of his finger. My father was ready for the touch.

This promise was to go unfulfilled. "Perhaps," my father thought

"I did not deserve it." My father was convinced that P.B. intended to give him a "mystic experience," something my father had hungered for as long as he could remember. His brother Bernard had had such an experience when he was sixteen (he called it "the great I am"—a sense of merging with the universe) and had been searching to repeat it ever since. It was what had initially drawn him to P.B. It was never entirely clear what my father understood by "mystic experience." It was to include some alteration of consciousness, some sudden "illumination" perhaps about the nature of the world, and especially, visible proof that the person was special—for example, had the ability to do something that ordinary people could not do. My father was not greedy: He did not want the ability to become invisible, to fly, to transmute base metal into gold. It would be enough for him if he could read another person's mind. He thought of this as something quite literal, like reading a page in a book. You had no idea what was coming next, you simply read. And the person would stare at you in disbelief and say: "It's not possible! I am thinking to myself, and you are repeating it thought for thought." In the mind of my father and P.B., it was no more of a miracle than the ability to read. For somebody who cannot read, to see a person speak words from a page seems miraculous.

It all made perfect sense, but Jack wanted proof. He wanted to see somebody, anybody, including P.B., *do* these things. "Mere tricks," P.B. would say. "Easy." Well, if they are so easy, thought my father, let him perform them. "I like tricks!" P.B. was well aware of my father's yearning. He knew that he wanted something that conjured up this world of mystery and power. The next day P.B. obliged, using his magic sight to look into my father's past life. He then told my father: "In your past life you obtained a higher advancement spiritually than you have now. You have yet to catch up where you left off." The attraction, the pull, was obvious for my father. P.B. knew what Jacques wanted. He wanted the feeling, or rather the *certainty* that somebody knew something about him that he did not know himself, and that this known something was positive and betokened a great future. P.B. said that he *knew* about Jacques's former incarnations—who he was, what had happened to him—and my father believed him. He was equally explicit about his powers to control other people's destinies. This was much more powerful, in the hierarchy of mystic powers, than the mere ability to hear what somebody was saying when they were not present or to see something far away. P.B. claimed that he had once had such powers.

P.B. told my father that he had been clairaudient and clairvoyant when he was eighteen. "I can project my astral body, too." "Well," said my father, "do you still have these powers?" P.B. smiled myste-riously and only answered: "I was told to stop it." "Why should I?" P.B. said he had asked. "Because," had come the answer, "there is something much higher awaiting you." My father was ashamed that he had doubted him. Of course there were higher things awaiting him. How childish of him to seek proof at this low level.

P.B. then told my father: "None of my Czechoslovakian students were hurt during the war. Only my enemies were put in a concentra-tion camp and died." The implication was that his students were protected. P.B. had cast an invisible shield around them, and while others died, they survived. Why, though, would P.B. have enemies in Czechoslovakia? my father wondered. And who were they? These are the kinds of questions my father quickly learned not to ask, for P.B. would go silent. Asking questions threatened to dry up the flow of information. P.B. then said, "Germany will produce some mystic now." I am not sure what he meant, but the fact that Brunton's enemies were put into concentration camps and died suggests that his enemies were Jewish and put into German death camps. Whom did he have in mind? Presumably Communists, since P.B. seemed to have an inordinate fear and hatred of communism as being "ungodly" and hence against mysticism, which meant against *him*.

P.B. exhibited a certain degree of healthy skepticism, which my father no doubt found attractive and convincing. He was always very concerned with my father's character, especially its defects. Even before they met, P.B. wrote to my father (on October 24, 1945): "You have greatly improved since your first contact with me but there are still serious weaknesses." The implication, for my father, was that P.B. had already exerted, on a level my father could not conceptualize, a benign influence.

P.B. seemed to have a great fear of insanity, in all its forms, and abhorred what he called "unbalanced" people, the fanatics, cranks, extremists, and monomaniacs who infested his domain of mysticism. Of Dostoevski, for example, he said that he was an "emotional psychopath" who "needed straightening out." He would never dream that he could possibly fit into such a category. He neither appeared nor sounded the least bit crazy. He would often criticize people for believing "myths" about mystics, for example, that Tibet was peopled with "adepts." "This is," he explained to my father, "mostly mythical." The "mostly" allowed him to claim later that there were a few, just a very few, and one of them, in fact, had been his teacher. This notion of a few good men is a common mythological theme. It is found in the Jewish idea of the "just" man and in other mystical traditions.

My father was fascinated by the notion of "occult" powers, but he was also a little bit embarrassed by the subject. P.B. was too. The topic came up often in their conversations. P.B. always dismissed them: Great yogis did not make such claims for themselves. But it was also clear that they did, or could, possess these powers whenever they wished. P.B. was interested in Helena Blavatsky, the leader of Theosophy, and seemed to think he had some mystic link with her. "I was born seven years after she died," he told my father, "we were both born under the same Zodiac signs," and she could "mentally access any book in any library in the world." It is not that my father believed such wildly irrational claims, but he was attracted to the idea that they were true and especially to the idea that P.B. knew about such matters. He had to have faith, he told himself. He not only told himself, P.B. told him too, often, as he wrote in his diary: "On the disciple's side there must be complete faith, devotion, loyalty, and a willingness to subordinate his own little ego, his own limited intellect, should they ever find themselves opposed to the master's guidance." It was easy for my father to believe that his own intellect was limited, and it was tempting to ascribe omniscience to someone else (P.B.). It is not just a form of modesty but a way of enjoying power vicariously. If P.B. knew everything, then Jacques, by being in his orbit, was exalted as well. Also, it was always possible that P.B. was testing him. Faith in the guru was essential. Each story served to intrigue my father further, to lure him with the promise that he, too, would soon possess these magic powers, have access to occult forces. Let it be at a lower level; it was only right, after all, that he start low. He was ready.

P.B. found the ultimate hook, the perfect way to enchant my father. On December 20, 1945, Paul Brunton had a "vision" about my father. Its content, as immediately recounted to my father, was to have an enormous impact on him for the rest of his life. As dictated to my father it was:

> You, Jacques, were seen in a vision looking about 10 years older than you are now. By that time your appearance had markedly changed. Your face was darker and the expression on it graver. You had developed some Occult Powers and when you looked at a person, you saw at once the inner state of that person, his character, mentality, virtues and weaknesses. Your reputation as a Seer was becoming increasingly known among the inner circles of Europe and consequently people would come to consult you from all over the world. You had entered into spiritual consciousness and had thus realized some of your chief aspirations. Your character was much purer, your lower nature was under control, and you were able to get messages from within very quickly. You reminded me in your manner and appearance of a medieval Kabbalist.

My father wrote down the vision as P.B. dictated it to him. P.B. corrected the text the next day. As he reread it, he thought that other disciples, especially Bernard, should they somehow happen to read the vision, would be jealous, and P.B. instructed my Jacques to change the account to the third person, calling himself "Althodas." "I had no doubt in my mind," my father recently told me, "that the vision did appear to P.B. I would be realized. It was a very great upheaval in my life, this vision, knowing for certain it would be fulfilled. I was absolutely convinced the vision was true and would come true. I prepared myself intellectually, deciding that if people came to me, I would never ask for monetary remuneration. I even kissed P.B., I was so exalted. He was very undemonstrative, however, and did not like that at all."

Althodas, P.B. told my father, was the name of a medieval Kabbalist, of whom my father was a reincarnation. (The name actually came from one of Marie Corelli's pretentious novels that P.B.—along with Queen Victoria—liked so much.)

The ability to read another person's mind is a popular favorite in Hinduism. Whenever I met a "spiritual" person, the first story I was likely to hear was how that person's guru could read thoughts. Ram Dass in his book *The Only Dance There Is* tells of meeting his guru, Neem Karoli Baba, in 1967 and immediately being told what his thoughts were from the night before. The guru has a powerful means of control over his disciple's thinking if the disciple believes the guru can know what it is he is thinking. Would one ever dare to think a heretical thought? Even if it were true, it would be an extraordinary invasion of a person's privacy.

My father felt "protected" by this spiritual father as he had never been by his real father. They were in almost all senses polar opposites. My father's father, Henry Moussaieff, later Henri Masson, was a large man, over six feet tall, noted for his physical strength as well as the strength of his "animal" passions. He liked to drink and to eat, and he liked surrounding himself with women he found pretty. There was a menacing aura of sexuality around him: He openly lusted after his daughters and was not opposed to using his own sons for his sexual pleasures either. He was also a violent man. My father tells of how a cat once scratched him, and his father closed the door, got a large stick, and beat the cat to death, to the absolute terror of his fifteen-year-old son. My father was small, delicate, and sensitive. Both as a child and as an adult, he abhorred all forms of physical violence, developed a great love for animals, and would never dream of harming them. He clearly longed for a gentle father. P.B. was in many ways that ideal.

In Indian spirituality, the master/disciple relationship is patterned quite consciously (the very word *guru* also means "elder") on that between father and son. On January 17, P.B. told my father (who wrote it down in his diary): "Once the Guru accepts the Chela [disciple] it is for a lifetime. Even if the Chela turns murderer, the feelings of the Guru towards the Chela do not change. If the Chela leaves the Guru, he can always come back knowing the Guru is waiting for him. And if the Chela does not reach the Ultimate in this life, the Guru will be waiting for him next life. He has coached him for many incarnations and will continue until the Chela reaches the highest stage." It was the ideal way to speak to my father, making promises my father was eager to hear. P.B. was implying that he had brought my father to India in order to be with him, so his master could bring him to a higher consciousness, fulfilling the promise of an earlier incarnation. They were linked from a former life, was the implication of P.B.'s words, and there was work remaining to finish. Moreover, this work was of the highest significance; in fact, it was of cosmic importance. This was a hook that was hard, if not impossible, to resist, especially for somebody who longed so desperately for these qualities—that is, for connection to a higher power and a solution to the "meaning" of life in his own life.

Like all mythic heroes preparing to undertake a perilous but essential travel adventure, preparations of a spiritual kind were mandatory. "Purification" played an important role. This was something "practical" my father could sink his teeth into, something he could begin to work on immediately.

What P.B. meant by purification was quite clear: My father must rid himself of sexual thoughts. On the second day of their meeting, he told him: "Physical contact with women should be avoided. Otherwise, one picks up their bad karma and vibrations." P.B. did not want a sexual interest in women interfering with the more important master/disciple relationship. A few days later P.B. had a minivision and told my father: "A beautiful woman will offer herself to you. It will be your first test. The Overself will test you. All the evil influences you feel will be just a test." My father was to remember these and similar conversations many years later, when he received news of P.B.'s marriage. He was in Hong Kong, and my mother sent him a telegram. " 'How can God get married?' I thought," he told me recently, and said he became depressed for a period of time.

In preparation for his return to America, my father and P.B. went to Ootacamund in the Nilgiri Hills, a favorite retreat for the English to avoid the heat of the plains. My father felt this was a rare privilege, as P.B. told him, "You are the first person that has been allowed to spend so much time in my presence." My father was convinced he was proof of P.B.'s ideas, that they were taking on him, they were working. He felt he was in an accelerated spiritual movie. He was high. On their walks, P.B. would tell my father stories about the spiritual path and about the personalities of the spiritual movement—Blavatsky, Olcott, Leadbeater, Besant, Krishnamurti, and the Theosophical Society. He would tell him stories of the life of the Buddha, repeat mystic gossip, discourse on Bahai, Thoreau, Emerson, Walt Whitman, the adepts of Tibet, how he will eventually retire into a cave. My father was utterly fascinated. It was on one of these walks that P.B. warned my father about sexuality:

OOTACAMUND, FEBRUARY 6, 1946. *The Sexual Problem.* At a certain stage of the Path the Neophyte must go through a Gate. On each side of the gate there are two lions and he must wrestle with both of them. Only after he has mastered his sexual impulses will he advance further on the Path and will then obtain Occult Powers, not before. He must get rid of the problem at its base, he must meditate on it, think of all the bad side of it, sexual disease, attachment, uncleanness, etc. etc. and whenever sexual thoughts come to him he must fight them by thinking of their opposites. A married Neophyte must not abuse it either, and at a certain stage of his development it would be better if he abstained from it for a while. When one practices meditation he becomes very sensitive, and sex is a shock to the nervous system. He must conquer that problem if he wants to advance and obtain Powers. He must have complete control over himself and time will test him and see how far he has advanced.

"Why am I here?" my father asked P.B. on one of their walks in the Nilgiri Hills. My father recorded the answer: "The only reason that we are here in this world is to obtain Spiritual Consciousness, no other reason. The main thing is to purify one's character first. Only then can you advance on the Path." Purifying one's character meant to become more and more like P.B. This was particularly difficult for my father to do, since he did not resemble P.B. in any way. He was volatile where P.B. was steady; he was passionate where P.B. was detached. P.B. did not ascribe all character traits to the individual. Some, he clearly thought, were racial.

The last entry in my father's India diary reads:

FEBRUARY 27TH, 1946: Today is my last day in Ootacamund. I spent the whole day with P.B. He gave me his blessing before leaving. His departing words were: "Remember you shall not be alone any more. Your material and Spiritual life will change. Your Higher Self will protect and guide you. Take good care of yourself. The foundation has been laid. Your life will take a new aspect."

My father felt blessed and happy beyond description.

What was my mother's reaction while all this was happening? Clearly women did not play a major role in P.B.'s spiritual universe, except as temptresses to avoid or triumph over. Nonetheless, there were exceptions, and wives of important and wealthy disciples had to be accommodated.

My mother was born Dina Zeiger on September 9, 1918, on the outskirts of Vienna. She was one of nine children. Her father, Meyer Chaim, was fleeing from the Turkish army, in which he was expected to serve. At that time, Jews were given sanctuary in Austria by the Emperor Franz Josef. My mother's mother, Sarah Zeiger, was a strong-willed and determined woman who suffered the death of many children during her lifetime. She was not given to mysticism. When my mother was a year old, the family returned to Palestine, where they lived until my mother was six. Just before they sailed for America, her only brother accidentally drowned at the age of seventeen, a tragedy her mother never got over. The family moved to America in 1924.

My mother came from a large, tight-knit, Orthodox Ashkenazi (my father's family was Sephardic) Jewish family. Her father was a quiet, scholarly, self-effacing man. Her mother had a zest for life, as I well remember, even though by the time she arrived in the United States she had lost five children. My mother, second oldest of the surviving children, was regarded as extremely pretty and very intelligent, and she had a great sense of fun. She was always an outstanding student and very much wanted to continue on to university. She began college, but the family needed her to work and she dropped out after a year. It seemed to her a very alien world, Indian spirituality, to which my father was introducing her. "Forbidding and severe" is the way she describes it now. But she had been brought up to "follow her man," and she allowed herself to be introduced to vegetarianism, meditation, yoga, and gurus with seeming little reluctance.

She first met P.B. when he returned from India and came to stay with our family in Los Angeles in 1946. At the very first meeting, they spoke about spiritual matters. For my mother, it was the first time she had ever heard such things. My father fell asleep, and my mother and P.B. spoke far into the night. "He asked me: 'Would you be willing to give up your children for the quest?' I said I didn't know, but I didn't think so. I felt I had failed my first test. A short while later Linda was very sick, and I prayed to God to cure her. P.B. told me that I had made a promise to God that if he saved Linda, I would do everything in my power to stay on the path. He warned me that I had to keep that promise."

P.B. was clearly much taken by my father. If we look at the photo of my father and P.B. in India in 1945 (when my father was thirty-three and P.B. was forty-seven), the two look like friends. But the friendship was never acknowledged as such. My father was looking for a guru, and it is clear that P.B. conformed to his expectations and encouraged them but never entirely satisfied them. P.B. would later claim this was because he completely denied from the beginning that he ever intended to be anybody's guru. While this is not true, to judge from the contemporary letters I have seen, P.B. was obviously also divided. On the one hand he wished to be considered a guru—a potent, powerful figure like the men from his early books whom he so admired. On the other hand, he had had direct experience, in the ashram of Ramanamaharshi, of just how destructive this could be, both for the guru and for the disciple. What exactly happened between P.B., the Maharshi, and the Maharshi's brother is not known. But whatever it was—evidently P.B. gave interviews in the Indian papers about the Maharshi that the brother did not find satisfactory—it soured the relationship between all three men. The guru/chela relationship, like most romances, tends to end badly, with both sides feeling aggrieved, hurt, misunderstood, and misused. P.B. was later to claim that all he wanted was friendship and companionship on his quest. But his letters clearly indicate that P.B. also wanted to be considered a sage, a guru, a mahatma, a rishi, a spiritual teacher. Bernard and my father thought of P.B. as a highly advanced adept, an illuminated one. It is of course impossible to be a guru all by yourself; by definition, a guru requires a disciple. The two are coterminous. It is a *folie à deux*, where the "insanity" is controlled, submerged, and even sanctioned by society. Or some societies. It was easier to be a guru and a disciple in India in 1945 than it was in America, even in Southern California where my parents lived.

My father had gone to India as a young, somewhat immature man of thirty-three. He had had a childhood filled with loss and lack of love. P.B. offered him a new kind of permanent "home," safety, and a direction and meaning to his life: the Spiritual Path. My father was treated as if he were very special: P.B. had told him that kings, ambassadors, ministers, and wealthy industrialists were all trying to have an audience with him. And here was Jack, able to spend several months more or less alone with him. Why? P.B. saw signs of *specialness* in Jack. They had been guru and disciple in a former birth; he was given a private mantra; he was told secrets about other disciples; he saw divine light emanating from P.B.; P.B. had a vision in which Jack was exalted. In short, Jacques was convinced that he had found a living god, and this living god loved him and saw a magnificent spiritual future for him. Is it any wonder that this meeting changed his life?

Chapter Two

Fasting Along the Path

My father stayed in India for about four months, walking, talking, and meditating with Paul Brunton every day. He returned from India shortly after my fifth birthday a changed man. From now on, his life would be dedicated to spiritual matters, to the path. P.B. was his guru. Moreover, much to the thrill, excitement, and wonderment of my parents, P.B. had consented to live for some time in our house in Los Angeles.

It was not easy to have a guru in urban Los Angeles in 1946. Certainly, in our immediate surroundings, P.B. was an embarrassment. He was our family secret. Family here meant only the four of us, my sister Linda having been born two years earlier. My father saw us as "special," singled out by destiny to be disciples of one of the great masters of all time. But *his* family, apart from his brother Bernard, took it very differently. For them, P.B. was a joke, not because they saw through him but because he was so unfamiliar.

This was even more true of my mother's family. Unlike my father's family, who were protected by international roots from complete parochialism, my mother's relatives thought of themselves as American to the core. I can remember one of my uncles telling me proudly that he had never owned, and would never own, a Japanese car. "There is nothing foreign in my house," he boasted. Well, P.B. was foreign, foreign by birth, by appearance, and by his interests, and my parents were always afraid that one of their relatives would bump into him in our house and an unpleasant scene would ensue, with the inevitable questions: Who was this man? Why was he stay-ing with us? Why did we treat him with such reverence? We would be accused of retreating from Judaism. After all, we never attended synagogue. And wasn't our vegetarianism a form of fanaticism? And we had all those books about Hinduism and Buddhism around the house.

My mother tried to explain it to her mother one day: "Ma, he is a kind of rabbi." "Oh yeah," said my skeptical grandmother, whom I simply called Bubbi, Yiddish for grandmother. "He don't look very Jewish to me." Still, this did explain to Bubbi why we treated him with something bordering on worship. It did not help much with my skeptical uncles and aunts. My mother was one of four daughters, close in age and otherwise, except when it came to P.B. P.B., for his part, made it clear early on that he regarded all of these people— those who had no interest in him or his teachings—as "lowly evolved." I agreed with this evaluation.

After all, had not my relatives come to my father as a group to point out that I was much too small and thin for my age, and that surely this was because I was a vegetarian? My father finally silenced them by telling them that I was really a midget, and he was trying to keep it from Di, so please do not mention it again.

"Lowly evolved," he told me, to explain them. This was one of the stock phrases I can remember hearing over and over again from a very early age. It seemed to explain all the evil in the world— wanton destruction, murder, plunder, rape—all came about because those involved were lowly evolved. Actually, I never knew how liter-ally this was meant to be taken. I heard P.B. explain the phrase in sev-eral different ways, but the main thrust was that these people had not lived a sufficient number of lives. They were "new souls," was an-other way P.B. had of putting it. The opposite was an "old soul," or one "highly evolved." While the upper reaches of higher evolution were pretty much reserved for P.B. himself, anybody who met with his approval was branded "highly evolved."

P.B.'s use of the word *evolution* was idiosyncratic. He did not believe, for example, in Darwinian evolution. Once when I was in school and was learning about it for the first time (it is a difficult concept for a child to understand), I asked P.B. if it was true that man evolved from the monkey. "No," he said, "the race of apes came from a conjunction"—he did not like to use more explicit language—"of primitive man and female beast." I had never heard that in school, which of course to me just went to show how ignorant my teachers were and how learned P.B. was. Apes were a degeneration from man; man was not an evolution. "Anyway," he told me, "the monkey came after man, not before." I didn't get it, but I didn't get evolution either, and I didn't insist.

For my parents, being "on the Path" was primarily an inward matter, but it also had certain outward manifestations. From the time my parents first met him, P.B. was fascinated with crank diets of all kinds. He was vegetarian, but he carried vegetarianism further than most. He was unwilling to eat any animal product and periodically decided that only raw fruits or some other abstemious diet was the only spiritual way to eat. My parents went along with these diets, adding improvements and niceties of their own. For example, they were much taken with a book by a certain Arnold Ehret called *Mucousless Diet*, and another book whose title struck me the first time I saw it: *Don't Eat Bread*. For a period of time I was fed no bread or bananas, which had been two of my favorite foods. I can remember one summer afternoon, when I was five, I was not to be found in the backyard of our house, which was a block from the beach in Santa Monica. My parents ran down to the beach, where I loved to go, and found me rushing at the pigeons, competing with them furiously for the crumbs of bread being fed to them.

Like P.B., my parents were fascinated with dietary regimes stricter and more bizarre than vegetarianism. At one point they, too, decided to eat no cooked food; at another we ate only fruit. They read all the health-fad books as they appeared, books by Gaylord Hauser, and especially Bernard McFadden's *Encyclopedia of Health*, and moderated their diet accordingly. On Sundays we often visited various eccentrics from the health food world like Mrs. Richter, an old woman who at that time operated the only raw-food restaurant in the world and who lived on an exclusive diet of raw fruit and nuts. We found her, spry at eighty, in the branches of a large walnut tree in her front yard, where she lived in the tree home she had built herself. "Healthier," she explained in a word. To me, she looked wrinkled and ancient beyond calculation, but my parents were impressed, and for a while my sister and I were fed only fruits and nuts. Another time a visiting explorer came for dinner and insisted on making us milkshakes with olive oil. This time, we rebelled.

It sounds worse than it was, though. For one thing, these enthusiasms rarely lasted very long, sometimes just a matter of days. For another, I was always a welcome guest in my friends' houses, where I could indulge in "normal" food. Once, to my parents' horror, they learned that I was eating immense amounts of bologna, which I thought was some kind of Mexican vegetable, from the refrigerator of a Mexican friend.

While P.B. encouraged his disciples to be vegetarian and we complied, my father was after all French, and there was nothing quite like a good meal to him, meaning wine, meat, and rich sauces. Upon arriving in a strange town—our family was always traveling— P.B. would immediately begin scouting for a vegetarian restaurant: Could one be found, and if so, would it be sufficiently rigorous to meet his impossible standards? When he located a suitable spot, he would announce in triumph that we were very lucky that evening, for he had discovered the perfect restaurant. My father would go along glumly, and I can still remember him scouring the menu with shocked disbelief, and his mounting horror as he would see one raw-food platter after another arrive at our table. But in front of his guru, he would say nothing. I suspect that on such evenings, my mother had to later bear the brunt of his bad humor.

Such was the household I grew up in: My parents did not identify, from the point of view of religion or spirituality, with the Jewish faith in which they had both been raised. (Culturally, though, they *were* Jewish.) If asked, I probably would have said that they were Buddhist or Hindu. They were not sectarian, in that they did not entirely identify with any one single religion from the East. They were disciples of P.B., and he was influenced by Buddhism, Hinduism, and most especially by a philosophical school within Hinduism known as Advaita Vedanta. Unlike mainstream Hinduism, Advaita regards the entire universe as a figment of one's own imagination. Rituals, gods, reincarnation, karma, all of these staples of Indian religion are only true from "a lower point of view." Eventually, they must all be abandoned when the truth, namely that they are only "ideas," is realized. A somewhat watered-down version of this philosophy is taught at the Vedanta temples in the United States, and I was often taken to them on Sundays in lieu of synagogue or Sunday school. The one closest to us was in Hollywood, presided over by the chain-smoking Swami Prabhavananda, Christopher Isherwood's guru, about whom he has written an evocative memoir called *My Guru and His Disciple*, which, unlike this book, is in praise of gurus in general, and the spiritual life in particular, especially the Vedantic version of such a life.

I remember going up Ivar Avenue, climbing steeply from Hollywood Boulevard straight up to Franklin Avenue, to a small secluded nest of houses where there was a Hindu temple surrounded by little wooden bungalows. As a young boy I was struck by the gentle demeanor of Swami Prabhavananda's junior colleague, whose name I no longer remember. He had a sweet, almost melancholy way of speaking about Vedanta that made me wonder, a few years later, if he really believed what he was saying. He was very young. Like me, he was probably born to it; maybe becoming a Hindu monk had not been entirely his own decision, any more than meditating with P.B. had been mine.

In 1946, when I was five, we lived between Beverly Hills and downtown Los Angeles, in a Mediterranean-style stucco house. Down the street lived my best friend Buddy McDonald. Apart from the food I ate, or didn't eat, I was a pretty normal five-year-old, and at this early age, I think it was decided that I was still too young to be introduced to "the Path." Besides, I had a remarkably foul mouth for such a young boy. I remember falling off my bike when I was six and being taken to a doctor for stitches. It hurt so much when he began the procedure that I started yelling "Giddami di Hell, ye sonny butch," which he had no trouble understanding. I had no idea where these words came from or what they meant, but the doctor was so taken aback and so appalled that he refused to treat me on the spot, and my mother had to find another doctor to stitch me up. Afterward, as compensation for my ordeal, she took me to Sears and bought me a carpenter's tool belt, which I wore around my waist. As we came out of the store, a little girl stared at me and asked her mother who I was. Her mother said: "Why dear, you can see from his tools that he is a carpenter." "A real one?" asked the little girl in a dubious tone. "Oh yes, a real carpenter." I was extremely pleased and felt very self-important. I was a pretty normal little boy.

My father had a kind of natural restlessness that he claimed came from his nomadic ancestors in the Central Asian desert. He sometimes said that, in his blood, he was a tent-person accustomed to moving from one oasis to another. He certainly loved to travel. As I write these lines in 1992, my father, at eighty, is just returning from yet another trip to India. I don't think there has been a year in my father's life when he has not traveled either to Europe or the Orient. The next year, 1947, the family moved to Tucson, Arizona, for one year. Bernard and Ida rented a house, "the ranch," on the outskirts of Tucson, and P.B. moved in with them but spent most of his evenings at our house. My father was thirty-five, my mother was twenty-nine, my sister Linda was three, I was six, and P.B. was just about to turn fifty, my age today. One reason they chose Tucson was for P.B.; he wanted to live in retreat, and he found the desert conducive to spiritual thoughts. But an even more important reason was that, in the desert, everybody could more easily indulge in the one thing they all wanted to do very badly but had a hard time doing in the city: fast.

It is not surprising that somebody as abstemious as P.B. would discover fasting. Besides eating no animal products of any kind, he took no intoxicating liquors, no drugs or medication of any kind, drank no coffee (only tea, to which he was addicted more for the rituals than the taste, I think), and ate extremely little. But even that little was sometimes too much, and he would periodically engage in fasting.

He told my parents a series of "facts": Fasting cleanses the body of accumulated poisons and the mind of accumulated errors. It improves eyesight, "because millions of tiny capillaries in the eyes are choked by toxic debris." "Twisted inclinations" are eliminated. I think this was a reference to sexual desires. Certainly P.B. believed that a fast contributes to "liberation from passions." In P.B.'s view, certain foods stimulate sexual activity, and it was best to eliminate those foods from one's diet altogether: eggs, oysters, chocolate, and meat. "Superfluous nutriment" in general, he held, encourages sexual excitement, which may be one reason he ate so little. Spices, too, were bad, especially mustard, pepper, and paprika, which directly stimulate the sex organs. One odd reason P.B. gave for not eating meat had to do with the fact that animals that are killed and eaten by man owe their own existence to the sexual lust of their parents. He held that the lust permeates their flesh in an invisible psychic-magnetic aura. So in eating them, he maintained, we take in their sexual aura. He urged colon flushes and strong purges to help eliminate the waste toxins.

P.B.'s fasts, however, were fairly mild, a few days at a time, sometimes a week on just water, but rarely more. When my parents become involved in fasting, they did it with much more gusto—with a vengeance, as it were. They did two-week fasts, twenty-one-day fasts, and even forty-day fasts. Sometimes they went on fruit fasts, at other times grape-juice fasts (where they drank only grape juice), and most commonly, pure water fasts, where they took no food at all, only plain water. The rituals accompanying these fasts were as important as the fasts themselves. Since at the end of a forty-day fast a person looks like a concentration-camp survivor, it was important to conduct the fasts away from the prying eyes of neighbors. Tucson was to be the first of many such retreats, where, in isolated houses, they could indulge in what they knew most people would neither understand nor approve.

My parents read a great deal about fasting and its benefits. They decided, in 1948, to go on the ultimate fast, the forty-day water fast. This definitely took some courage, not to mention willpower. To the lay person, certainly to me now, it sounds dangerous. But my parents and other disciples would smile self-importantly at the naïveté of those who believed that the body requires food. They claimed that one could live for long periods without any food whatsoever. A fast up to ten days was considered easy. I think they believed that sixty days, however, was the maximum that could be attempted without injury to health. Unlike the Indians, nobody I knew as a child claimed to be able to live permanently on no food at all. This may have been, however, part of the underlying view.

Short fasts of a week on fruit juice, or grape juice, were common and carried almost no prestige. The major fast, the prize fast, to which everyone aspired, was the forty-day one. My mother did not believe she could complete it, but she began the fast with my father anyway.

The ultimate goal of the fast was spiritual benefit, but the more immediate result was bodily purity. Their mythology about the body held that in the ordinary course of eating, the body is necessarily poisoned. Fasting was the quickest way to draw out these toxins. This was a popular word among the "health conscious" in those days. The body was supposedly filled with poison from all the bad food consumed. It was necessary to periodically cleanse it of all impurities. All the spiritual people I knew were preoccupied with bodily fluids of all kinds, both those that go into the body, and those that come out of it.

My parents would prepare themselves for the forty-day fast by reading up on the subject (*Fasting, Vitality and Nutrition, Fasting and Grape Cure* by Edmond Szekely, Basil Shackleton's *About the Grape Cure*, and Herbert Shelton's *Fasting Can Save Your Life* are some of the titles I remember, and a book about fasting by Mahatma Gandhi), by discussing fasting benefits with other disciples, and of course by meditating and reading spiritual books. They often went to a place south of Los Angeles called McEachens, in Escondido, where they could fast hidden away from the rest of the curious world. My sister and I were left in the care of a housekeeper during these times. The two of us never fasted with them, with the exception of one three-day fast.

I found it a decidedly unpleasant experience that I did not wish to repeat.

The test was the tongue. My mother and father discussed the state of their tongues every morning the way other people discuss what they are going to have for breakfast. Generally a person's tongue is coated in the morning. This is a bad sign. My parents were ecstatic the day they awoke in the morning and could tell each other that their tongues were "pure," without any coating. For years I was encouraged to use a tongue-scraper, to remove the morning coating, even though to some extent this was cheating, since the purity should come naturally as a result of an inner process and not by adventitious methods. To my parents the clean tongue was the surest sign that the fast was taking, that it was creating benefits. The nature of the stool was also carefully monitored, for color, consistency, smell, and so on. It was once explained to me that vegetarian animals, like horses and elephants, do not have stool that smells. The purer we ate, the less our stool would smell. They were looking for external signs of purity. The idea was that being pure in body would make it easier to be pure in spirit.

My parents were both keeping a fast diary, in which the state of the tongue, the stool, and of course weight were all noted and annotated. Weight was never the real issue, but it was carefully written down, possibly as proof that there was no cheating. It was considered elementary knowledge that actual physical hunger would cease after a few days. I am not sure this is true, but in any event hunger was considered of minor consequence, since it is purely physiological. To conquer the body was certainly good, but the real enemy was the mind. The mind had to be conquered. It was backsliding if thoughts centered on food and its preparation. So diary entries would often say: "Did not think of food once today!" except, presumably, in writing the entry itself. As the body became clearer, the mind, too, was supposed to clear up, and both the physical and mental energy level were to rise.

My mother began her fast on April 23, 1948, when she was thirty years old. She kept a diary:

5TH DAY—10TH DAY: Getting stronger all the time, not to the extent of very great physical activity, but feeling very good. Take early morning sunbaths—do quite a bit of mail for business and personal every day and much reading and much activity of the mind. Am beginning to marvel at the miracle of fasting and cannot conceive why it is not used more for the sick civilization that is all about us. Probably have to evolve to such great knowledge. It is truly my Higher Self and Power aiding me. Took enema today 10th day and passed quite a few hard little clumps of feces, natural color no odor. Sleep well every night from 9 P.M. arising by 6 A.M.

My mother gave up the water-only fast after twenty-one days. But then she "felt badly" and decided to continue for another week: "Broke fast on orange juice on Friday, May 21, after 28 days—eating cherries, apricots, melon and yoghurt for three days. Have gas. Natural bowel movements in morning. Feel good."

My father, however, was determined to fast the entire forty days. Nothing less would make him a spiritual hero, and only thus could he possibly expect the ultimate benefit that he was always, and eternally awaiting: spiritual enlightenment. Meanwhile, his weight was dropping and dropping, from 140 when he began to 92 pounds toward the end. Eventually he was confined to bed, like Kafka's hunger artist. Why was he not more alarmed, more insecure about the medical risks? I am not certain. An air of urgency and significance hung over these endeavors, and I think for my father the fast was a means of forcing the hand of the spiritual powers. The fast, he hoped, would produce the concrete, material proof of the spiritual progress that he was waiting for. He too kept a diary:

STARTED FASTING ON APRIL 14, 1948 AT NOON. 2ND DAY: Felt weak but went downtown on errands which weakened me further. Tongue not coated. No movement. Pulse 62. Slept well all night. 3rd day: Very weak. Reclined most of day, too weak for anything. Looked very skinny, sunken eyes, face drawn. 4th day: Very weak, stayed in bed most of day. No energy whatsoever.

5th day: Slept well. Mentally active. Weight 110 pounds. 9th day: Feel better and out of bed most of day. 19th day: Feel better, tongue not coated. Took enema. Few feces. Slept from 10 to 3 A.M. Felt refreshed. Mentally very alert. 21 day: Took enema, was surprised to see a few feces. Also took pictures. Went to a movie. Weight: 102. 22 day: Tongue much cleaner. Breathing better. Urine much clearer. 25 day: Feel hungry. Took watermelon juice [cheating!]. It did not agree with me. Tongue heavily coated. Felt bad all day. 28th day: Pulse 45. Slept well. Had very symbolic dream: Steep hill, could hardly make it— finally made it to top of hill. Probably signifies that I will achieve my goal of spirituality and good health only after struggling very hard for it. Exact weight: 101 lbs. What I did on 28th day of fast: Called Ahmed in New York, bought one star sapphire for $1000, made arrangements for a $5000 letter of credit for Ceylon goods. Spoke to P.B. in Croton. He told me to break the fast on yoghurt and have no roughage after the fast. Apple sauce, purées, no salt (he explained why). Little cheese. No vegetable fiber. He said that spiritual results will show later and finished by saying: "God bless you." He is sailing for England in 36 hours. Ordered $2000 worth of cultured pearls from India. Went downtown shopping, bank, wrote business letters, etc. etc. 29th day: Nothing but a little water. Felt good. Slept well. I have had no sex urge at all during fast, only one night emission. May 14, 1948: Exactly one month of fasting. Pulse 48, temperature 96. Weight 97 clothed, 92 naked. Felt very weak especially in the afternoon as I had to go downtown to mail some special delivery valuable packages. Nothing but water. No stomach pain. Left kidney hurts. Tongue coated but not too much. No bad taste in mouth. I look like a shadow of my former self. 36th day: Feel better, stronger. I sleep about 3 hours at night, mind extremely active, transacted large business by mail and phone. Tongue still coated.

On May 9, 1948, in the middle of this fast, my father wrote to P.B.:

This is a different Jacques that is writing to you today. Certainly not that weak sick person you saw after 5 days of fasting. It is truly amazing to see the increase of strength and how well I feel considering it is now my 26th day of fasting. My mind is now so active I awake as early as 2 A.M. and do not need any more sleep after that. I intend to continue after the 40 day fast with mainly raw food with which to build a vital new bloodstream. Diana is also getting on very well after her first three days which were also weak days. She is now on her 16th day and intends to go on to complete a 21 day fast. She also requires much less sleep, arising in the wee hours of the dawn and is very active. It is a revelation to us both, never having known such mental activity, and have become voracious readers. Yesterday I weighed 101 pounds fully clothed and am quite near the skeleton stage.

Two weeks later, on May 24, 1948, my father continued his account to P.B.:

Today I am very and extremely happy to write I have finished my 40 day fast, although in the strictest sense of the word it wasn't a complete fast, as after the first 10 days of nothing but water I did resort to a weak dilution of orange juice. Of course after talking to you over the phone, I stopped that mixture and substituted diluted grape juice and watermelon juice. Anyway, today I have completed forty days, and now I am having some yoghurt and some pureed fruits which I will continue for a while. I am feeling well but of course still a little weak. However, my physical appearance is on the haggard side, with my face sunken in, but I'm not worried as I know this is only temporary. I want to thank you for having planted the seed that resulted in my taking this fast, as otherwise I never would have been able to do it. Now the report on Diana's fast. After 21 days she proceeded to break her fast, but her best instincts would not allow her to and with the help of a still persistent headache she decided to follow her inward urge and continue fasting (that is, also the weak dilution of orange juice with water) until all trace of headache, etc., left. She had to continue for 28 days in all. Since this is Diana writing I shall switch to the first person here. I am feeling very well and am very happy I undertook this fast and of course most happy it is over, since it is not too pleasant. I am looking forward to spiritual benefits after a bit and shall resume my neglected practice and study of the Path. Talking to you before your departure inspired both of us a great deal and we thank you so much for your blessings.

Even beyond food, the most dangerous of all spiritual snares was sexuality. My father's sexuality was anything but dormant at the time. For if my father's appetite for food disappeared during his fast, evidently his sexual appetite did not, despite what he told P.B. and his diary. I know this from later conversations with him.

The whole purpose of the fast was to create purity of spirit. Pure in spirit meant many things, but the thing it meant most often and most importantly to P.B. was sexual purity. P.B. spoke about sexual purity constantly and seemed to have no sexual appetite himself. Or so he said. I don't think my father ever asked him directly whether he ever felt anything so impure or mundane as sexual desire, but certainly my father believed firmly and with no doubt that P.B. did not.

Sexual purity was easy to define: It meant no sexuality whatsoever in thought or in act. At least this was the goal. P.B. recognized, of course, that telling this to a young married couple was likely to be counterproductive, so he modified it. Married couples should be abstinent for as long as possible.

As he told my father on one of their walks in India, P.B. believed that "lust" (a very bad word in P.B.'s vocabulary) belongs to a man's "animal physical inheritance, and it *must* be brought under control and discipline." Sexual desire was a "lower" instinct and had to be conquered before progress on the spiritual path could be considered. The way to do this was to engage in sex with less and less frequency. Fasting seemed the ideal time for abstinence. So my parents, as they later told me, had almost no intercourse during their fasts. P.B. encouraged abstinence among his married disciples, once in fact suggesting that my parents spend two years without sexual inter-course. But if the appetite for food was easily conquered, the sexual appetite proved far more elusive and cunning.

Once my mother was over her fast, she set about looking for domestic help. She placed an ad in the local paper, and soon a stunning (so says my memory and my father today) twenty-one-year-old blond and blue-eyed aspiring actress named Martha answered the ad. My mother was interviewing Martha when they happened to pass the room where my father, in the last days of his fast, was confined to bed. Suddenly revived to an astonishing degree, he jumped out of bed and told my mother, "Hire her immediately!" Surprisingly, my mother obliged. Martha, whose fiancé was away in the service for one year, was hired on the spot, and she moved in with us the next day.

P.B. often told my father that the disciple is frequently tested by his guru in odd and unexpected ways. Most of these tests were for the purpose of seeing if the disciple was worthy of the master. But there were also larger, more generic tests, provided by the higher powers, to see if a disciple was ready for progressing on the spiritual path. Shortly after Martha was hired, P.B. said to my father: "I think you are getting closer to illumination. A test is bound to be at hand. I think it will take the form of a sexual temptation."

Although P.B. had met Martha, Jack was thunderstruck: How could the higher powers know that this was indeed what was going on in his mind? Ever since Martha had arrived, he could not stop looking at her, and she was evidently not adverse to flirting with him. She took showers outdoors where he could see, and she knew he was looking at her with something bordering on devotion: "Everybody loved her," he told me recently. "How could you help it? You loved her, my father loved her, I loved her. She was the perfect woman, healthy, a beautiful body, she went to bed with a smile and woke up with one. Everybody who came to the house wanted to take her out. You loved to stroke her hair. She adored you." Could he make a deal with the higher powers? He was prepared to renounce intercourse if they would accept fondling. Maybe if he did not go below the waist—just the breasts? He decided this was acceptable and proposed it to Martha. She agreed, and he began fondling and kissing Martha's breasts. I don't know if I saw this at the time or if I learned it later, directly from my father, but it did happen, as my father now confirms. My mother, on the other hand, tells me that this is merely a wishful fantasy on my father's part. "Martha was not that kind of woman," she told me recently.

Sexual abuse, whether of employees or children, occurs in many contexts, but a spiritual household offers the perfect cover for it, as if deploring something is the same as avoiding it. Paradoxically, I think, it even promotes the abuse. P.B. said he disapproved of sexuality; maybe abuse would have been unthinkable to him. But he created an atmosphere, I believe, in which it could flourish: one of secrecy, charged power, hierarchy, and a refusal to acknowledge what was actually taking place.

Martha played a role in my sexual life as well, not entirely dissimilar to the one she played in my father's spiritual tests. When my parents went out one evening, Martha asked me to come into her bedroom. She was on the bed, dressed only in her underpants, or perhaps it was a see-through nightgown. I was wearing my pajamas. She asked me to sit on her bed, and she began talking to me about her boyfriend, and how she wanted to get into the movies, and did I think she was pretty, and she didn't know if she really loved her boyfriend—talk of that kind. I was fascinated. At ten o'clock at night, she turned on the radio to listen to her favorite program, something called *The Inner Sanctum*. It was a horror show and began with the frightening sound of a door slowly opening and an announcer saying: "Open the creaking door." I was terrified. This amused Martha, who told me to come into her arms and hold on to her if I was frightened. I was, so I did. I know it felt good. I have a vague feeling that I was assigned some specific sexual task, perhaps encouraged to surreptitiously rub up against her genitals, and possibly she did the same to me. I cannot really remember the details. She told me this was our secret, and that if I never, ever, told my parents, she would let me come whenever they went out and listen to this program with her and hold her whenever I became scared.

I remember some sort of code word I was expected to use to signal what I wanted. I knew this was a forbidden game, and I did not tell my parents. I wanted it to continue; I did not want to do anything to jeopardize the sexual pleasure I got from it. I also liked the fact that whatever we did, it was never explicitly acknowledged. As I look back on this incident from the vantage point of having written about the sexual abuse of children, I know this was unmistakably sexual exploitation. But I cannot remember feeling anything other than sexually aroused and thrilled. Perhaps if the first time one feels sexual feelings directly, it is in a context of abuse, the violation is transformed by the arousal, so it is not felt as violation. Abuse becomes sex. Possibly boys learn to boast rather than to admit helplessness. "Fixation" is not a concept I favor, but I can see how a certain attachment to secrecy and surreptitiousness developed from this early experience. For some time this was a necessary component of sexual excitement for me; "cheating" was exciting.

Now I know that whatever she was engaged in with me, she was also involved in sexual acts with my father. This produces, today, an odd sensation of something quite awful going on—in *her* mind, at least. Did this "sharing" of my sexual life with the sexual life of my father, even as we shared a spiritual life in which sex, not to mention sexual abuse, was denied, have repercussions on my later sexual life? Might I have known about his involvement with her? These are all speculations, but she was using me in a way to which she had no right. I was not hers to toy with.

I have just found a note I wrote her on January 6, 1949 (my father dated it!), when I was eight. It is bizarre:

My own Martha Deir.

Look Martha how about you and me haveing a conversation huh come on wonsh you please do it my swyt huh my puny lille half-pint. Good by. Your good boy Jeffrey. Love Love Love Love Love

In reading this note, which I did not remember and had never seen until now, I was suddenly reminded that "puny little half pint" was a phrase Martha used of me. Coupled with the vaguely sexual and ominous "please do it my swyt," it suggests that more went on than I now know. This is probably why I only remember the pleasure. It sounds as if humiliation were the more likely emotion at the time, but one I changed into arousal, making it impossible for me to recollect. "Conversation" might well be the code word she devised for me. It does not sound like the word of an eight-year-old boy. On the other hand, my sister Linda remembers listening to this radio program at least once or twice with me and Martha. Perhaps Martha used our being all together as an excuse for later being alone with me. It was just something we all did. Perhaps, too, though unlikely, I am mis-remembering. This is, not unexpectedly, what my mother thinks.

I now believe that this kind of abuse is inevitable in an atmosphere where physical desire is either denied, ridiculed, or feared, while power is worshiped and physical access unquestioned. The fact that these thoughts—not to mention deeds—were in such conflict with the spiritual life the disciple was supposed to be living made it even sexier, or led to intolerable tensions, depending on your point of view. The "sexiness" could not even be thought about, and the tensions could neither be acknowledged nor discussed. Such "temptations," including the temptation to pursue the only sexual outlet the prohibitions allowed—abuse in secret—seemed so foreign to P.B., so far removed from his life. At a conscious level, this is no doubt true.

It also seems possible that the abuse was one factor that made the spirituality so appealing. With sexual abuse, authority is all that matters, power is all that is real. Spirituality offered a nonintrusive authority and a seemingly benevolent power. With sexual abuse, secrecy must be maintained. Our spiritual life was an exciting secret, one of charged, shared meanings. Both sexuality and spirituality offer transcendence of the mundane. But spirituality offers a child dignity and control that sexual abuse takes away. It even promises a replacement for, and an end to, sex itself.

Did P.B. know he was living in a hornet's nest of sexuality? With all his talk of purity, and all his prohibitions, did he in fact help create it? Could this possibly—horrible thought—have been one of the ways that *he* found sexual excitement, by controlling everyone else's sexuality?

P.B. often said that the fact that most human beings make their paradise depend on the mere friction of paired bodies is something marveled at by planetary visitors. Presumably, beings from other planets, visiting earth in disguise (I think he meant himself), are amazed and repulsed by sexual intercourse. He also said that the philosopher (again, himself) finds wisdom only in total abstinence, and that voluntary celibacy within a marriage leads to peace and strength.

In fact, as he told my father in India, P.B. had an entire series of reasons for discouraging intercourse among aspirants: "1) One's karma becomes entangled with that of the other person. 2) One becomes infected with low thought-forms hovering in the other person's aura. 3) It is retrogressive, not evolutionary. 4) Each time a person who practices meditation engages in intercourse it disintegrates something of his achievements. With the lowly evolved, it gives a special shock to the nervous system." He also claimed that children born to parents who rarely practice intercourse are markedly superior in every way. P.B. told my father that he and other questers would "have to choose between abject unreflective surrender to a biological urge, grotesque over-evaluation of a glandular excitation on the one hand, and freedom, peace, and security on the other." No wonder my father developed ulcers.

I had no idea what kind of world we were living in, outside the spiritual one that permeated our home. As it happens, my father was having financial difficulties at this time. It pained him to turn to P.B. for "mundane," that is, nonspiritual advice, but he felt it was urgent. He sat down with P.B. and explained his entire financial situation to him, including a full disclosure of his present impasse. P.B. thought silently for a long time, and then spoke:

"Jack?"

"Yes," my father said, eagerly leaning forward, the better to capture these words of wisdom:

"There are only two solutions: Earn more, or reduce your expenses."

My father was deeply disappointed and said he could not help but be reminded of the French phrase *"Cinq minutes avant sa mort il vivait encore"* (Five minutes before his death he was still alive), an expression for belaboring the obvious.

I was profoundly ignorant of the world around me. What I knew about the Second World War, or any other major event in history, could have been exhausted in a sentence or two. I don't think my parents subscribed to any newspaper. They certainly never encouraged me to ask questions about politics or current events. This would have been an insult to P.B. and his concern for eternal rather than mundane matters. But in another sense I actually had a life apart from the "spiritual" realm.

It was 1952, I was eleven, and I loved to hike in the hills above our home in the Hollywood Hills. How many homes does a child have? One, I suspect. This one was mine. It was where I collected polliwogs, built a pond, cultivated a garden. I loved to race off after school with a band of friends to an abandoned quarry and hike around. One afternoon I persuaded Larry, Jerry, and Jan, my "gang," to go there; but only Larry, my ever-faithful companion, would follow me up the steep cliff. About five hundred feet up, the shale loosened and Larry and I were left stranded on a small ledge, unable to go either up or down. Larry began to cry. Finally, I yelled to Jerry down below to run for help. A half hour later the firemen arrived, along with the press and our mothers. The firemen lowered one of their companions on ropes, and we were hauled up to safety. The next day, Saturday, April 5, 1952, the *Los Angeles Times* ran the following story, my first appearance in a newspaper:

FIREMEN RESCUE BOYS STRANDED ON 500-FOOT CLIFF. Firemen in a dramatic two-hour rope rescue in the Hollywood Hills late yesterday brought down two small boys marooned on the side of a 500-foot cliff. The rescue was accomplished by Cpt. Vernon Breadon and Frank Gorman of Truck Company 27. While the mothers of the boys watched anxiously from below, three firemen atop the steep bluff slowly lowered Breadon and Gorman on ropes to where the youngsters, imperiled by sliding shale, clung to the canyon wall. The young adventurers, who decided to try scaling the cliff on their way home from school, vowed afterward that they'd never try again. They are Larry Slater, 9, of 5715 Spring Oak Drive, and Jeffrey Masson, 11, of 2534 Park Oak Drive. Their homes are not far from an abandoned quarry which is frequently used for movie scenes. The steep cliffs, pocked with caves, rise almost vertically from the floor of the quarry. The mothers, Mrs. Diana Masson and Mrs. Erwin Slater, breathed sighs of relief when the boys were hauled to safety.

The front page of the L.A. *Daily News*, too, shows photos of two ordinary, grateful little boys. But while I was on the ledge, I was chanting Sanskrit mantras to protect us.

In September, when I was still eleven and my sister Linda was eight, my parents left for Europe on an extended trip, for about three months, I think. It was the first time Linda and I had ever been separated from them for so long. My father's sister Vicki and her husband, Avram T'homi, came to stay with us at our home in the Hollywood Hills. I liked Avram, a romantic figure who had been commander-in-chief for Jerusalem in the Jewish underground army, the Hagannah. He was intimately connected to the founding of Israel and the struggle against the British right after the Second World War in Palestine. The stories he told us had to do with adventures in the real world, a secular world, and I found them exciting. Vicki, too, was lively, skeptical, and completely unspiritual. She was a Communist and a dancer and was a lot of fun. She had no hesitation in debunking P.B. and everything he stood for. I think there was a certain amount of friction in the family because they so obviously disapproved of my parent's obeisance to P.B. My loyalties were of course with P.B.; nevertheless, I could see the appeal of a different kind of world.

My parents returned from Europe in May 1953, with my father announcing to us that he had "retired." I was not sure what he meant, but he told us that he wasn't going to work anymore, and we should all get ready for a long vacation in Hawaii. On June 26, 1953, my mother wrote to P.B.: "We are all leaving for Honolulu on the 29th of June by United Airlines and expect to remain there two months. The kiddies are looking forward to this vacation, and are very excited, as they have never been in a plane before." I was indeed very excited. I adored Hawaii. I suppose it was my first concrete vision of paradise. We lived on the beach in Lanikai, and I often swam to a small island just off the coast. We all liked it so much that we decided to spend one year there with P.B. as our guest, in 1954.

Our house had a pond in the garden filled with turtles. I had a boat, and friends. I loved going to school barefoot, where I was the president of the eighth grade. (My slogan for the election capitalized on my smallness: "The little guy with the big ideas.") I loved coming home to take my motorboat on exploratory trips to the little islands close by. I am struck, in looking at scrapbooks from the time, how "normal" I appeared. *The Windward Reporter*, the local newspaper, said this: "These are the students you picked as your students of the semester. In the eighth grade division, Jeffrey Masson came in unanimously. Jeff lives with his parents, Jack and Diana Masson, at 838 Mokulua Drive. He's president of the eighth grade class, and also secretary of his home room. Asked about his grades, he said if it's possible, not to have them published. If that's the case, they merely must be good. He likes swimming and is very active in sports. He is well liked by his friends, teachers, and especially popular with the opposite sex. Quite a guy." But I was not just the little guy with the big ideas; I was the little guy with the secret guru. This is the life I never talked about outside of the house.

I don't think I was ashamed or embarrassed, though it is difficult to know from this distance. I only knew that having P.B. live with us was a special privilege that other people were not to be told about. I knew, too, that P.B. thought the world was hostile to him and his ideas, and he discouraged us from speaking about him, or telling "outsiders" that he lived with us. Cogent or viable alternatives to the life I was living were ruled out by this secrecy. Whether that was disturbing to me then, as it ought to have been, I cannot now say. Every impulse I had to live like others was countermanded in the house. I was, in fact, popular with girls in my school. But I knew that this was not well regarded by P.B. Other stirrings were even less acceptable.

*   *   *

P.B. did not approve of any physical demonstrations, and particularly not of a sexual sort. I knew this, and I knew that on this road, I was headed for disaster. I can remember one day in Hawaii in 1953, at twelve, playing hide-and-seek with a neighbor girl. Crouched in the garden shed together, I found my arms around her waist. Without realizing what I was doing, I put my hand between her legs. She giggled and squirmed and told me it felt good, before running off. The physical feeling was totally new to me. I can still remember clearly her face and how she looked at me. I must have connected those feelings I had for her with P.B.'s frequent condemnations of sexuality: It was the ultimate example of being "caught up in maya," a cosmic illusion. "You cannot simultaneously be on the path and engage in sex" was what P.B. had said. Sexuality and spirituality were mutually opposed. You could not have both. This was disheartening to my father and frightening to me, as I began to have a sense of what he was referring to.

But if sexuality was forbidden, it was also highly visible. The topic always seemed to come up in conversation. I don't know if this was P.B. or my father, or both, but for a man who claimed never to have any sexual desire, P.B. certainly never tired of engaging in conversation about sex. The conversations revolved around spiritual disasters caused by sexual desire. How a guru had revealed himself to be a hoax by sleeping with a disciple, or how a disciple (invariably male) had destroyed his chances for spiritual advancement by giving in to a sexual urge. He knew of many instances and told them with great gusto. We all listened, a little sheepishly, but fascinated.

I had some vague sense that spirituality also somehow tied into unusual bodily practices. We had taken one of P.B.'s poorer disciples as a housekeeper. Her name was Margo, and she was a health fanatic. The bathroom and her room in our house were filled with little yellow bottles, and with a curious smell that for some time I could not place. It turned out that she believed drinking and bathing in her own urine was the cure for all current and possible diseases. Her boyfriend was a weight-lifter, and I often found them locked in an embrace on the living-room couch. P.B. did not approve. He did not like the sex, and he did not like the urine. He abhorred what he called "unbalanced" people or fanatacisms of any kind. It obviously never occurred to him that his own views would ever be seen in this way.

The combination of spirituality with intense (if sometimes negative or eccentric) preoccupation with the body was part of the world my parents inhabited. When I was thirteen or fourteen, I learned that we were not the only ones. Staying at the Algonquin Hotel in New York, my sister and I were in the elevator, discussing something to do with Buddhism, when an extremely tall stooped man entered. He joined in our conversation, asked me what book I had in my hand, then brought it up to his face to examine it more closely. I remember thinking he was totally blind. He was not, but nearly. He told me that bad eyesight could be cured by something called the Bates method without the use of glasses. I remember thinking that he was not a particularly good example of the truth of his belief. We chatted some more, and he said he would very much like to meet the parents of two such unusual children. We proudly took him up to our room, where he introduced himself to my parents as Aldous Huxley.

My parents attempted to convince Huxley that they knew a guru—not P.B.—he should visit in India, and he clearly looked as if he knew that he was incapable of making such a visit. I could not take my eyes off his and noticed that each time he wrote something down—names of books and gurus—he brought the paper to within an inch of his eyes.

I was disappointed with the conversation. I think I was expecting Huxley to acknowledge P.B.'s preeminence in the "perennial philosophy" and that my parents and he would trade spiritual war stories late into the night. Huxley, after all, was a great admirer of Hinduism and especially of Vedanta. I wanted to hear more secret doctrine, feel that I was in the presence of a sage, for I knew that P.B. admired Huxley. But I felt no such thing, and it occurred to me, albeit for only a fraction of a second, that perhaps we were all mistaken, we had *all* been taken in. A gigantic hoax had fooled us all, even—terrible thought—P.B., the master himself. Such thoughts, however, were intolerable.

Chapter Three

Meditating to Illumination

During the years that P.B. lived with us, meditation was the most serious and important of all household activities, the essential element of our spiritual life. Meditation sustained P.B. as sex and food sustain other people. He lived for it. He talked about it constantly. He wrote about it. He practiced it for long periods, every day. It was considered a very special privilege for a disciple to be invited to meditate with the master. The main spiritual advantage of having P.B. live with us for long periods of time was that we all got to meditate with him on a daily basis. Meditation was usually in the evening, before dinner. This was a solemn occasion, for it was really only during meditation with the guru that one could have a transcendental experience.

P.B. was not without a sense of humor, even when it came to meditation. But his highly developed sense of humor was almost entirely confined to making fun of people who laid claim to spiritual powers they did not possess. He loved to ridicule other gurus who believed in the supernatural. He thought this crude. I never understood, and do not to this day, how he differentiated their beliefs from his. Not infrequently a rival guru—all other gurus were rival gurus—would visit the house. After his departure, my parents and P.B. would spend happy hours dissecting the absurdity of his beliefs, his naïveté, crudity, and ignorance.

P.B. did not like rivals. He abhorred "cranks," a word commonly spoken in my family but reserved for others. The fact that their own relatives considered my family and especially our guru as cranks was too absurd to even contemplate. P.B. often told us that the true sage spoke and behaved without any quackery and without the tone of pontifical infallibility, so that when "questers" as he called them (those on the Quest for Truth) came to see him for advice, they were helped without all the mumbo-jumbo of the usual guru. P.B. insisted on speaking in simple language. But we were not to mistake the simplicity of his language for a lack of depth in his thought, or even to falsely believe that we were at the same level. P.B. explained that he could gauge the truth of *any* situation better than could the disciple, since the disciple's vision was clouded with ego, and the ego of the ordinary man was constantly caught up in the net of desire. P.B., we all believed, was entirely without desire.

"The impact of my aura will gradually strengthen, calm, and uplift any sensitive disciple," P.B. told us. Certainly he believed that in his presence there were healing vibrations that had miraculous healing powers. P.B. said there was nothing miraculous about these vibrations; it was merely the innate tendencies born of former incarnations that are beneficially influenced by the healing association of an adept. He didn't actually say "I am an adept," but it was hard to mistake the gist of his words. We all wanted to be more and more like him.

I can remember my father putting his two hands together, standing straight, and looking very solemn and calm when P.B. walked into the room. After all, he did not wish to appear insensitive. In fact, my father and I did everything we could to imitate P.B., with no apparent success. P.B. was the expert on everything; at least, his opinion counted more than anybody else's. My father encouraged this by asking P.B. a constant series of questions and acting as if the answers came from God. P.B. was duty-bound to answer—how could the guru not know everything?—but I think that sometimes playing the part of the guru became wearisome even for him. This might explain some of his desire for solitude.

P.B. somewhat reluctantly allowed my father's cousin Shimmy to meditate with us. In this important ritual, P.B. would fold his legs in the lotus position (easier for him than for many people because of his diminutive size), let his arms rest over his knees with his forefinger and thumb forming a magic circle, and begin by chanting the Tibetan Buddhist formula *Om Mani Padme Hum* ("Hail to the jewel in the lotus"). He would chant this Sanskrit mantra in a deep and resonant voice, allowing the *Hum* to echo for perhaps a minute. An altogether impressive performance, learned in India.

Shimmy too was impressed and determined to imitate the master. So one evening, during meditation, after P.B. chanted, Shimmy began to chant the same mantra, but he did so in a squeaky falsetto voice, mispronouncing the words and losing his breath before the end. P.B. could not contain himself and burst into laughter. He had a hearty laugh, and once he got going, he could not be stopped. My father and I joined him, and soon we were all three rolling around on the floor in a paroxysm of laughter. What made me laugh was simply the performance itself. But for P.B. it was more serious: a disciple was laying claim to the privileges of a master. Shimmy was deeply humiliated and never attempted to chant again.

I was always a little bit nervous about pretending to have knowledge, especially spiritual knowledge, that I did not really have from direct experience. I wanted so much to be like P.B., just as Shimmy did. I also wanted to please the adults around me. I wanted to make them proud of my spiritual abilities. But I feared I had none. At some level, I *knew* I had none, I simply didn't know that this could be a normal thing, even a good thing. Instead, I was always afraid of embarrassing the adults around me and of being humiliated myself.

Once the actor John Hall, who played Tarzan after Johnny Weismuller, visited us in Hawaii and insisted on hypnotizing me in front of our guests. I was given a posthypnotic suggestion—when he spoke the word *cloud*, I was to leave the room and bring him an umbrella. I was fully conscious and totally unhypnotized and only frightened that I would forget the cue and bring down embarrassment on our guest. As it turned out, I acted as expected and then blushed scarlet at my deviousness. How can adults believe this rubbish, I remember thinking; I was equally embarrassed for John Hall and my parents. The fact that I knew my parents were skeptical (they asked me after the guests left whether I was pretending and I admitted I was) protected me to some extent from entering this make-believe world entirely. This was true in general. My father was a very shrewd businessman, requiring a certain lack of fanaticism for financial success. You could not be too gullible and expect to make a profit. So while my father totally believed in P.B., he was less easily taken in by other matters. His skepticism, however, never encroached upon his complete certainty in P.B.'s stature as a mahatma, a great sage.

My mother was less inclined to complete surrender to P.B. For one thing, she was immensely sociable. Considered a very pretty woman, she derived great pleasure from the way she was perceived. She loved to have people around. She flirted and laughed and enjoyed herself. Others responded positively to her. For P.B. and my father, this was merely proof of her being "caught up in *maya*," a phrase often hurled at me as well, as the ultimate insult. In the spiritual atmosphere I grew up in, the *real* world was called maya, "illusion," while the illusions were considered ultimate reality.

The goal of all P.B.'s disciples was to have an "illumination," that is, an intense mystical experience that puts one in touch with a "higher power." My "illumination" came when I was thirteen. I had been meditating with P.B. for some years, more or less daily when he lived with us. I found it hard to stay still for the thirty or forty minutes that a meditation usually lasted. P.B. never moved. My mother coughed constantly, whether from boredom or nervousness or for spite, and my father gave her looks of annoyance.

For my thirteenth birthday, just around the time of my bar mitzvah in fact (my parents remained culturally Jewish in spite of their spiritual allegiance to P.B.), P.B. said that I could have a special meditation with him. I determined that no matter how uncomfort-

able I became physically, I would sit still and not break my concentra-
tion. Usually what I thought about during meditation was what could
possibly be going on in the mind of P.B. Where was he? Was he, too,
thinking, like me, about other people and what they were thinking
about? Impossible, I thought. He was, I was certain, lost in some kind
of supramundane, otherworldly experience. He was, I was absolutely
convinced at the time, in an altered state. This time, as usual, I
was thinking about all these things. My legs began to hurt, my eyes
burned, my arms were tired, my skin itched, and I longed to stand up.
But I persisted—and it paid off. For soon everything began to feel
better, and I could actually feel myself entering a kind of altered state.
No doubt the rhythmic breathing helped. It was the first time I had
ever felt anything like this, and I was ecstatic. It did not last long, but
P.B. seemed to sense it and asked me afterward whether I had felt
anything special. I told him I had. He said he had known it, and that
this was my illumination.

It was not entirely unlike my earlier experience with hypnosis: I
could not help but feel that I was fooling everyone. I *wanted* to believe
that something out of the ordinary had happened to me; it made
everyone, including me, feel so happy, not to say exalted, and very
special. While I had definitely entered some sort of "altered state,"
altered need mean nothing more than that it was in some minor way
different from my ordinary state. I was willing myself with all my
might to "have an illumination." It was expected of me. It was the
right time. The circumstances were right. I was with the right master.
It was really up to me. It would have been churlish not to experience
something around this time. If it had been a pretense on my part, as I
often guiltily thought it was, at least it was for a good cause. P.B. may
have been all-knowing, but perhaps I could somehow get around his
omniscience and make him, my parents, *and* myself believe that I had
achieved the first major goal of the aspirant.

Through my "illumination," I was now definitely considered to
be on the spiritual path. My parents seemed suitably impressed. Even
my father, whose main complaint, after all, was that *he* had never had
an illumination, seemed more pleased than jealous, although it made
me nervous, especially since I knew my illumination was falsely

acquired. I was treated, from then on, with a new kind of respect. I was a little guru in the making. I can't say that it gave me no pleasure, or that I was displeased at the whiff of power a guru could command, even a little one. I can remember embellishing the experience itself with each telling, until I had just about convinced myself that I had seen the face of God. P.B. and I were both rather pleased with ourselves.

I was thirteen years old. With both my bar mitzvah and my "illumination" behind me, I was beginning to feel more and more like an important little man. It was time I learned something special. What could be more special than Sanskrit? Sanskrit, I had always been told, was the language of the gods, the ancient sacred language in which all the very texts that P.B. revered were written. I assumed, as did everybody else, that P.B. had completely mastered the language. As I later found out, this was wrong, but in any case, P.B. knew a teacher, Judith Tyberg, who was dean of studies and professor of Sanskrit and Eastern religions at something called the Theosophical University in Point Loma, California, which I strongly suspect now had no more than a handful of students and a smaller number of teachers. She lived in Glendale, in a house that also served as the Sanskrit Center and a bookshop. When we returned from Hawaii, I called her, made an appointment to see her, and the next day arrived on her doorstep.

    An elderly woman answered. "Hello," she said, "I'm Judith Tyberg." I was invited into her house, and ushered into a sitting room that was filled with Oriental art: Buddhas, rugs, Tibetan tankas on the walls, incense burning. I felt right at home. The room smelled mysterious. I loved it. Dr. Tyberg herself seemed to me ancient and very serious. Within minutes she told me that "Sanskrit is truly the mystery language of the Aryan race, the divine language. It is the instrument used by high initiates [yet another term for masters] to impart Truth to men [sic] in the early days of our Fifth Race." I didn't really know what she was talking about (what on earth was a Fifth Race?) since all her terms came from modern Theosophy, something I knew nothing about. (Theosophy is a system of mysticism founded in 1875 by

Helena Petrovna Blavatsky and continued by Annie Besant, drawing heavily on Indian "wisdom." Tyberg had gone to Benares to learn Sanskrit so that she could understand the Sanskrit words used by Blavatsky in *The Secret Doctrine*, an incomprehensible book written in 1888 that she tried, wholly unsuccessfully, to interest me in.)

Tyberg had written her own book in 1940 called *Sanskrit Keys to the Wisdom Religion*. In fact, this book was nothing more than a list of five hundred Sanskrit (and Tibetan) words from the major Theosophical texts. They were not really words, but Theosophical concepts, and I found them difficult to memorize. But when Dr. Tyberg decided to teach me the Sanskrit alphabet, I perked up. We had our first lesson a few days later. I could not believe I was learning this wonderful and strange new alphabet. I felt important. I could not have been a more eager or better pupil. Each word I learned seemed pregnant with spiritual meaning. Sanskrit appeared to be such an exalted language. No words struck me as trivial. Of course, this was because Tyberg was not teaching me to hail a cab in Sanskrit, but to read the Sanskrit scriptures. Or so I thought. Actually, I learned much later that Sanskrit is a language like any other, and that if you want to buy vegetables, or write a thank-you note, or sing nonsense syllables, you can, theoretically, do so. The language is there for you to do as you wish with it. Most people who say they "know" Sanskrit simply mean that they have learned a series of discrete words, much as the modern American will find a series of Sanskrit words in *Webster's Unabridged*, like *yoga, sutra, shastra, ashrama, mantra, karma*. To know these words is not to know the language. No matter how many thousands of these words you know, you are no more capable of reading a sentence written in Sanskrit than I was able to read French because I knew all the words to Edith Piaf's love songs by heart. Sanskrit has a grammar, a syntax, and a secular history like any other language.

I also wrongly thought that Sanskrit is not read or spoken but chanted. The whole language, I assumed, was one vast mantra, a spiritual chant. My education was being channeled toward the solipsistic notion that everything that happened to me had a purely spiritual purpose, and nothing secular was of any value. I and my

spiritual companions were all that mattered, and here was our
true language. I was being offered a language that made "ordinary"
thoughts seem unworthy. I was on the guru track.

By now I was considered mature enough to help P.B. in his work,
especially since I had learned to type in school. So that same year, I
became P.B.'s "secretary." I was thus finally in a position to answer one
of my own questions: What did P.B. do all day? He was living in a
small apartment in Santa Monica. I loved taking the bus to his house
and being able to smell the sea breeze as the bus got closer and closer
to the ocean.

My first job was to go through his rather voluminous correspondence and cut out any bits of blank paper that he could use for making
notes. Even enough space for a single line was systematically kept.
This included envelopes. P.B. also wanted me to transcribe and then
file hundreds of scraps of paper on which he had scribbled notes or
taken down quotations from his reading for use in his own books. He
was a voracious reader of any book on mysticism. He knew stories
about almost every mystic who had ever lived. Although I didn't know
it at the time, his most recent book, *The Spiritual Crisis of Man*, published
in 1953, was to be his last. I was sure that I was helping to type his next
magnum opus. After I transcribed these endless notes, I would file
them away under topics of my own devising. I have no idea how he
could ever have found them again, since my system was entirely
idiosyncratic. Nonetheless, when I read his *Notebooks*, I recognized
some of the entries I had made.

My other task was to unravel many yards of string that had
come to him on different packages. He kept them all and would often
ask me to link two or three smaller pieces into larger ones. This
seemed like such an inordinate waste of time that I couldn't help
wondering whether it wasn't a test. He was extraordinarily frugal in
other ways, however. He did not like to throw away paper towels.
After using them, he would lay them out on his little balcony to dry
for use a second and third time.

P.B. lived not only a frugal but also a very abstemious life. His
small apartment was almost bare, except for absolute necessities. The

refrigerator contained little except one or two tomatoes and a carrot: lunch and dinner. He drank nothing but water and tea. There were no books, either. He explained that he kept his "library" in storage. I was never to see it and often wondered if it really existed. The only thing he had in abundance was tea.

At least four times a day, P.B. would call a tea break. It was one of his obsessions. He had special teas from all over the Orient: Japanese green teas, black tea from China, Lapsang Souchong, and especially jasmine tea. The water had to be extra hot. He insisted on putting the loose leaves (he abhorred the idea of a tea bag) in a wooden holder for infusion and then in a little earthen pot. He drank young hyson green from Cathay or Taiwan for breakfast, semiblack oolong for midmorning, and smoky kapsan or flowered jasmine for midafternoon.

"P.B.," I asked him once, "why did you get upset when I brought you the Darjeeling tea from my parents?"

"I have given up these stronger teas."

"Are they bad for your health?"

He smiled mysteriously. "Well, yes, but that is not why I don't drink them anymore."

I really didn't care why he preferred one tea to another, but I asked him why he didn't drink strong teas anymore and was utterly fascinated with the explanation he came up with:

"There is a fifteenth-century Chinese poet who drank only the mild tea that was produced from the tea leaves grown in Cathay."

"Yes?"

P.B. smiled.

"You mean, you are the incarnation of that poet?"

"Yes."

This kind of "knowledge" that I got when I stayed with P.B. seemed to me in such contrast to the knowledge I got in school. At the time, I thought I was immeasurably fortunate to learn about P.B.'s earlier incarnations. But I was not entirely certain how I was meant to put this knowledge to use. And to tell the truth, I was more interested in learning about who *I* was in former incarnations than who he was. Moreover, the snippets he gave me never added up to anything useful, never explained anything. I wanted these esoteric bits of knowledge to point to something significant, to explain some mystery. Instead, they always felt unsatisfyingly incomplete, like the spiritual gossip P.B. so much enjoyed, just interplanetary chit-chat. It would be years, however, before I could recognize this.

P.B. never made it entirely clear from where he derived his knowledge. He rarely openly stated anything; he preferred to hint. So when he told me that people who speculate too much on former births can develop hallucinations, I was left to infer that what *he* did when he spoke about former births was not speculation. The notion that P.B. was hallucinating was risible. *We* speculated; *he* knew. He seemed to know everything.

Once I asked him about the reincarnated life of plants:

"P.B., do plants eventually become animals?"

"Yes."

"Well, how many times does something have to be born a plant before it can enter the animal kingdom?"

"They cannot be counted."

"Aren't there laws?"

P.B. smiled. I sometimes heretically thought he smiled mysteriously when he simply didn't know what to say.

"And after we are animals for a long time, we become humans, right?"

"Correct."

"What if we're really bad? Do we go back, in the next incarnation, into an animal body?"

Maybe he thought I was worried: "No, Jeff, the transmigration of souls from human to animal bodies is a fiction." But then he seemed to reconsider: "Still, while rare, it is not impossible." How exciting to think that P.B. knew the answers to such strange questions. My imagination would soar when I talked with him like this.

I knew that P.B. loved pet animals, as I did, and I wondered what their fate was, especially that of my cocker spaniel. And so while working for him one day, I asked him, "P.B., will Taffy be reborn with me in her next life?"

"When Taffy dies," P.B. told me, "her invisible spirit will hover around you. She will be fully conscious, and as far as she knows, she will still be in her usual world. She will think you are petting her, and be happy. Yes, she will reincarnate with you, but as a higher animal." I couldn't imagine anything much higher than a dog.

"Do all the planets have beings who reincarnate on them?"

"Yes."

"Are there any beings from other planets here?"

"Living entities come here from less evolved planets. And we eventually go on to higher ones. But this has to be done within certain limited periods. After that, the possibility of entry ceases. Normally, animals don't need much of a rest period between births. Humans, though, need many years of rest." How much P.B. knew! What a joy to ask all these questions and be given such certain and precise answers. And yet how disquieting. Was it really all true? Was it at all possible? I was never entirely without the germ, at least, of skepticism. I rarely gave voice to it directly, sensing that it would not be well received. There was really nobody, at this time, to whom I could turn for an alternative view of the world.

"Can we choose where we incarnate?" I asked him.

"To some extent. If you love a race or an individual strongly enough, you will be drawn into its orbit when reincarnating."

Why, then, I wondered, had P.B. not been reincarnated in India, which he seemed to love? I was glad, though, to think that I had chosen to live with my parents. I liked the idea of having had some choice in the matter.

Where did all this knowledge, which I could not learn from my schoolbooks, come from? It had to be direct experience, I thought. But I could not understand why he would not answer *all* questions so directly. Did he know? I always assumed it was the nature of the question that determined his answer, not the limitations of his knowledge.

Once I asked him how he knew these kinds of things.

"I know it from intuition."

"Are emotions involved?"

"Not at all. What is important are spiritual and moral values, and metaphysical capacities and spiritually intuitive qualities. It is these values that contribute to my knowledge. Emotions have nothing to do with it." P.B. seemed to have a horror of feeling something. At other times P.B. told me that he knew what he knew by "revelation," that most mysterious of entities. What exactly, was a revelation? I was never to find out.

"Can anybody know it this way?"

"No, most people depend on intellect and emotion. Jeff, the difference between savage and sage may be only two letters in the alphabet, but two thousand incarnations." He meant that the sage had reincarnated thousands of times, the "savage" but a few. It was all very neat and simplified, spiritual science fiction for children and adults alike.

He was the sage. Was I the savage? No—and this was my salvation—I was the companion of the sage. I was blessed. I could not believe my good fortune. P.B. encouraged this budding elitism. He spoke constantly of the elect, of the special, of the privileged. Even though he believed these privileges had been won by hard toil in previous incarnations, he definitely subscribed to a stratified hierarchical worldview. Social justice and equal rights were foreign to his temperament, as they are to any mystical system. P.B. wrote explicitly: "Since all men are obviously not equal, it would be unwise to give all men equal rights." He also wrote that "we must accept *and submit* to the World-Idea with its ascending hierarchy of creatures and preestablished order of things."

Every evening, I would go home and tell my parents about the wonderful day I had spent with P.B. They would look at each other significantly, as if they knew about some deeper purpose to all of this. I felt I was unbelievably fortunate to be in the presence of this great man and that all the trusted adults in my life were in agreement about this invisible world of power and meaning with which P.B. in particular was on such intimate terms. How could they all be wrong? Perhaps if I had spoken about it more openly to my teachers, friends, or relatives, I would have been given another perspective. But to do so would have been disloyal, a sign of weakness. How could I doubt the word of God?

I did once ask P.B. why other people could not be told the truths he knew. He told me we had to be tolerant.

"Remember, Jeff, we were once at the same level that they are on now. The notion of rebirth teaches us tolerance. Do not despise those of obvious inferior intelligence. Think of their internal age. They are still young. Young souls."

I never really did, consciously at least, doubt that P.B. was speaking the truth from direct experience. I think I quickly stifled any notion that he was simply inventing it all. But however briefly and stillborn, this heretical idea occurred to me. Something always felt a little odd.

One afternoon when my work was finished, P.B. invited me to take a bath with him. It never struck me as unusual until this moment, as I recount it. I remember the incident well and cannot recall anything sexual about it. We were about the same size then. I was very small for my age, short and slight. I remember thinking: "So it is possible to be small yet great." P.B., too, was conscious of his tiny stature. I was surprised, looking at his genitals, that they so resembled my own. I suppose I thought that God, naked, would look different from his creatures. I also noticed at the time that he, too, was circumcised, which puzzled me, since I did not know then that he was Jewish. Actually, I felt quite proud that he had invited me to bathe with him; it seemed like a special favor, a mark of distinction. How many disciples got to bathe with their guru?

That night, when I told my parents, they looked at each other with what I thought, at the time, was a look of pride. It seems odd to me now that it didn't occur to them to be concerned at a grown man asking a thirteen-year-old boy to bathe with him. But on the other hand, our whole family took baths together, regularly. Even as an adolescent I can remember bathing with my mother, possibly until I was sixteen. The family was considered special and therefore exempt from ordinary rules. If I ever objected, which I sometimes feebly did, I was asked: "Are you ashamed of your body?"

"Nobody else does it," I would say.

"Do we have to be conventional, like everybody else?" The flip side of P.B.'s "no sex" rules was the sexually charged atmosphere around our house. Purification and sexuality were not just opposites; they were fused in a dance of denial.

Earlier, when we were younger, my mother had insisted that we children take enemas, given by her. My sister flatly said no. I went along. This continued, I believe, into adolescence. It was meant as a health gesture, a means of purifying the body. I don't remember it as sexual, but memory or no memory, it was of course a form of bodily invasion. Cloaking sexuality in spiritual covers may have disguised the underlying sensations and the real meanings, but it did not eliminate them. A spiritual family could not abuse its children; therefore whatever happened in that family, it was not, it *could not* be, sexual abuse.

Chapter Four

Reincarnated from Another Planet

Of all the conversations I had with P.B., the ones that seemed most to fire my imagination had to do with other planets and with reincarnation. I think, now, that P.B., like Judith Tyberg, was in fact much influenced by Theosophy, and particularly the writings of Madame Blavatsky, in which reincarnation plays a major role. But in my eyes at the time, he was just telling me things *directly from his own experience*. I had no inkling that he may have been repeating ideas he had read about. Most of his ideas came from India, and in Indian philosophy reincarnation is taken for granted. I cannot think of a single Indian philosophical tradition that does not accept the reality of reincarnation as too fundamental even to argue. It is simply stated as fact, whether in Buddhism, Hinduism, or Jainism. What is compelling about the theory is that death is only an interim event, a moment in one's personal history.

Exposed to the idea of reincarnation as a child, it was difficult not to think about it, even if only imaginatively. Who had I been? With whom had I been associated? To whom had I been married? Who were my mother and father? Brothers and sisters? Friends?

What did I do? And especially, what had I done wrong, for which to-day I am suffering the consequences? Particularly for a child, who is trying to figure out who he is and where he came from, reincarna-tion offers an easier and more complete explanation than one em-ploying more complicated or critical or social or psychological factors for how we came to be who we are. If it was not ultimately convincing, it was certainly compelling.

P.B. immersed himself, and the rest of us as well, in discussions of reincarnation on a regular basis. For him, and for me at the time, they were hardly fantasies. They were reality. So I took it that P.B. had memories of his earlier existences. Indeed, I remember when I was fourteen or so, walking on the beach with him in Lanikai, on the windward side of Oahu, early in the morning. We both got up at dawn and often took walks together. We were watching the crabs racing for their holes, when I asked him point-blank:

"P.B., do you remember your past lives?"

"Of course," he replied, looking somewhat astonished.

"All of them?" I persisted. He hesitated for a moment, perhaps taking in the enormous implications of an affirmative answer.

"Not all, but many."

"Well, how many?"

"Oh, quite a few."

I was not to be put off: "But how many were there in all till now?" I think I was beginning to irritate him, for I sensed that he was about to change the topic, and I dearly wanted to hear more about reincarnation. It is not that he was ever reluctant to speak about it, but perhaps a concrete answer to such a clear-cut query would have risked raising more troubling questions.

"Tell me about one," I quickly said.

"Well, not long ago I was sitting at my desk, writing out a sen-tence from a Chinese classic, when I suddenly realized that I was the very person who wrote those lines more than two thousand years ago!"

Though I was deeply impressed and suitably awed, I felt com-pelled to ask, because I really wanted to know the answer:

"But how do you know that?"

P.B. answered in words I was often to hear: "I have reason to believe so." But it was this reason that I wanted. Always, whenever it looked as if we were getting to the bottom of some topic, P.B. would either resort to silence or give me and everybody else the impression that somehow he *had* to be elusive, mysterious. He simply *knew* more than he could possibly reveal. The world he lived in was highly charged, heavy with mysterious, secret, potent, even deadly forces.

"Can you remember my past lives, too?" I wanted to know.

"No, I cannot remember them, but I can remember some of mine in which you played a role." This memory business was tricky for me. What exactly did P.B. mean by "remember," and why was it that other people could not remember their past lives? According to P.B., everybody had past lives, but of course not everybody could remember them. Especially unable to remember them were people who did not believe in them. But why was memory so selective this way? If I can remember something from my past, I cannot claim that such a thing is impossible, or could not happen. Even if skepticism dictated that such events were unlikely, if I *remembered* them, I would choose to suspend my skepticism and trust my memory. So among the many hundreds of millions of people who had past lives, but did not believe in the existence of past lives, surely *some* of them would remember these lives *in spite of themselves*. But none ever did. And those who did, amazingly, always came from within the ranks of those who just happened to believe in the existence of reincarnation, or were raised in societies in which belief in reincarnation is a staple of growing up. Actually, in terms of population, those societies probably outnumber the rest of the world.

But here P.B. was touching on a topic that could not fail to ignite my most passionate curiosity: *my* past lives. He knew who I *was*. "Well," I persisted, "who was I in your incarnation?"

"We were once fellow monks together, in ancient Egypt."

"Yes, yes," I said, urging him on. But that was all he was going to tell me. The mysterious smile appeared, and I knew this foreshadowed the end of the conversation. But why? Was the memory only a faint, dim glow? Again, I could not help but be fascinated by this thing he called "memory of past lives." Not only did I not have it, I could not imagine it, and I could not imagine how one got it.

"P.B., how can I remember my past lives?"

"Most people cannot, fortunately, remember. It would be most distressing if they did. Imagine all the awful things that have happened to you."

I did. He was right. Still, I wanted to know if it could be done.

"Yes," he explained, "in meditation, in time, with practice, it could come. I will give you a series of exercises that will help." And indeed he did give me some breathing exercises, and some obvious mnemonic devices, like trying to remember the earliest memory I had, and then pushing memory to go beyond that, to my actual birth, and then even beyond. But it never worked. My earliest memory at that time was from when I was five or six, and try as I might, I could never get beyond that. I could *imagine* what had happened earlier, but I could not remember it. I did not remember my birth, and I knew nobody who remembered theirs. I could certainly *imagine* what had happened to me in a former life, but I could see no way in which it would be possible for me to *remember* what had happened in it. None of this, however, made me skeptical. The existence of past lives was a "given" in our family, a staple of dinner-table conversation. We talked about reincarnation and past lives the way other families discuss Super Bowl Sunday.

What I could never understand, and still do not, is precisely what relationship reincarnation had to the existence of beings on other planets. One day when I was fifteen, P.B. and I were sitting in my room next to a little shrine I had prepared, with statues of the Buddha, incense from India, Sanskrit sayings, and other odd things for a boy to have in his bedroom. I decided to ask him, because I knew that P.B. believed that there was life on other planets as well.

"P.B., were all your incarnations on *this* planet?"

"No."

"Is life on other planets similar to life here?"

"No, other planets are inhabited by higher beings."

Higher beings!

"How come they never come to visit us?"

"We are not worthy."

"But they could come to talk to you and your disciples, couldn't they?" I asked, hoping he would take the hint. The mysterious smile again. He knew something he could not tell me—I hoped it was that they were on their way. I would sit in my garden at night, looking up at the stars, and watch for the spaceship that was bound to come soon. How much P.B. could reveal to our space scientists if only he were willing to talk! Why, the mystery of whether there was life on other planets could be solved in a single conversation with him! All he had to do was tell the scientists the truth.

Once, in Los Angeles, walking to the observatory in Griffith Park in the Hollywood Hills, I asked him: "How do you know for certain there is life on other planets, P.B.?" His answer was all a young boy could ask for: "Because I have lived on another planet." There it was! I knew it all along: Higher beings lived on other planets; P.B. was a higher being; P.B. came from another planet. He was not speculating, he was remembering. But if he "came" from another planet, there was the mystery of how he got here. This exercised my imagination for quite a long time. Since I knew so little about P.B.'s early life, I was not certain he had actually been born here. I asked my parents about this mystery, and they seemed a little puzzled too. Evidently P.B. did not look kindly upon questions about his early life. He simply refused to answer. My parents really did not know where he had been born, nor to whom. I was therefore not certain that he had been born at all. Maybe he came here fully formed, straight from the other planet.

I asked him: "Did you come from another planet before you were an adult?" He did not answer directly, but he told me that he had had personal experience with UFOs, both saucers and ships. I imagined he was telling me that he had come on one of these ships. He also told me that "the move was a foolish one. I was very tranquil there, and here my life is troubled." He looked pretty tranquil to me here, too, thanks in great part to my parents' spiritual and financial devotion, but I imagined some blissful tropical paradise on Venus where all he did was sit on a cosmic beach and meditate next to a cosmic ocean. Was he alone, I wondered? Had others come with him? I asked him.

"No, I am alone," he answered. "But superior beings came to this planet ages ago. They completed their work, and they left. There are visits from time to time from different parts of outer space."

Just as I had hoped! P.B. was receiving visitors from outer space. If only he would let me meet them. But to ask seemed impossible. After all, I was not a superior being, I was just an ordinary boy from this planet—although an ordinary boy fascinated by the notion that beings from other planets were visiting my father's guru in our own house. I assumed they were not just paying a social call, a chummy visit from old friends back home. No, there was probably a purpose to their visit, vastly important work needed to be accomplished. What was the nature of this work?

"*Nothing*, Jeff, is accidental," P.B. told me often. "Everything is preordained." The universe was very orderly, in P.B.'s view. "Higher beings are listening to us all the time." I had a vision of giant TV screens on another planet on which all our conversations were being recorded and filmed. The secret visits must have been a result of such monitoring. They *knew* what was happening here in the immense detail that no one human could know. An interplanetary benevolent plot was afoot to save the world from some enormous catastrophe. What was that catastrophe? I was not to learn for several more years, though clearly it was the motivating force behind many of P.B.'s most mysterious gestures from the early 1950s on.

What did P.B. really believe about himself? I think that at some point he became convinced that he had indeed come from another planet. This is an unfamiliar variation on a familiar theme, known to psychologists as "the family romance," where a person, unhappy with his parents and his current position, imagines that he comes from some exalted lineage, usually royalty. P.B. was later in life to drop hints to other disciples that he was from another planet. In volume eight of his *Notebooks*, he writes: "When after the act of dying I shall be carried away to my own star, to Sothis of the Egyptians, Sirius of the Westerners, I shall at last be happy."

There is no question that P.B. believed not only in the existence of other planets with people living on them, but that these other planets are more "advanced" than ours. Already in 1935, in *The Secret Path*, P.B. had written: "For Christ descended on earth from a superior planet, which was His real home, and which is far ahead of ours in spiritual consciousness." In his *A Hermit in the Himalayas*, written a few years later, he says explicitly that Sirius is inhabited by superior beings:

> The beings who people it [Sirius] are infinitely superior in every way to the creatures who people Earth. In intelligence, in character, in creative power and in spirituality we are as slugs crawling at their feet. The Sirians possess powers and faculties which we shall have to wait a few ages yet to acquire. They have detected our existence already, when we do not even know and often do not even believe that the star-worlds are inhabited.

P.B. implied that he came from Sirius, and here he says that Sirius was a superior star, peopled by supermen, that is, people like himself. But he rarely said these things in any direct way. Why the hints, the allusions, the mysterious smiles? Was he afraid of being taken for insane? I think so.

In addition to being an expert on reincarnation, P.B. claimed to be a great authority on death and dying, and not in any academic sense, either. He *knew*, he always said, from direct experience. I don't know if he was referring to his memories of former incarnations, or to the fact that he had visions about it, but he was insistent. He knew *exactly* what happened after death.

"P.B., what happens when a person dies?" I asked him one day.

"The body is discarded, but the mind remains."

"Does the person know he is dead?"

"No, many times they think they are still physically alive. They can see others and hear voices and touch things just as before."

It sounded creepy to me. "What happens then?"

"The mind will go through many different experiences, and then will sleep for a long time. When it awakens, it will be deeply refreshed."

"What kind of experiences will the mind go through?"

"Everybody is shown what he has *really* done with his earth-life, what he *should* have done with it, and what he *failed* to do with it." That was frightening, even for a little boy with not all that much life behind him.

"Can anything be taken along?"

"No, nothing. You cannot take anything with you at all, no object, and no person or personal relationship."

"Will I be all alone?"

"No, when you die, you will vividly see a mental picture of your master, and he will guide you safely into your new existence. He will explain it and will reassure you. Because it will be very new and unfamiliar to you." I assumed he meant himself, and I was much reassured. It was a great comfort to believe that P.B. knew all about death and what happened after death, and that he would be with me.

In the fall of 1953, P.B. was traveling in Europe. On October 23, my father wrote to him: "Omar Garrison, a writer for the *Daily Mirror*, is writing a series of articles on Pseudo-mystics in Southern California. He spent a few years with Mahatma Gandhi in India. He and his wife are coming to our house for dinner tonight. Jeffrey is beginning to show quite an interest now in The Path, and we have started him with spiritual novels like *Brother of the Third Degree* which impressed him greatly."

I remember that dinner party. We were living back on Park Oak Drive in the Hollywood Hills, and I was about twelve. I was instructed to ask Mr. Garrison the following question, and I remember it well, because I had to memorize it carefully: "Mr. Garrison Sir, do you believe in metempsychosis?" (a pretentious word for reincarnation). I cannot remember his answer, but I know that it was the basis for the discussion that followed. It was also what allowed my family to bring up the subject of spirituality, while giving them first some idea of how their guest would react (you never knew when you might be in enemy territory). Although P.B. was not at this particular party, he almost always attended these functions incognito; that is, he would be present because it was considered "research" for him, but for reasons that he never made quite clear, his identity was not to be revealed.

P.B. did not want to be recognized in public. I could never understand what he was afraid of. Suppose he were "recognized"— what possible effect could this have on him or anybody else? But in any event, he insisted that we never introduce him as "Paul Brunton, the author," but always as "Philo S. Opher." P.B. called himself a philosopher, using the word in a rather archaic sense of a man pursuing or having wisdom. We were "questers"; he was a philosopher.

When it was absolutely necessary to introduce P.B., I was instructed to slur over his name, say something indistinct in the hopes that nobody would ask anything further. If that seemed unlikely, then I was instructed to say, as did my parents, "A friend, Mr. Opher." "Glad to meet you Mr. Ofer, what line of work are you in?" P.B. never came up with a satisfactory answer to this obvious question. The less people knew, the better, as far as he was concerned. He would be as vague as possible and immediately change the topic. He did not wish to be "discovered." It was as if he were on a secret mission. Moreover, from his point of view, what could he say? "I am Dr. Brunton, from another planet, reincarnated to save you and your ilk from deep ignorance"?

In 1955 we were together in Rome for a week's vacation, and my mother, P.B., and I decided to go to a movie. P.B., though, was afraid he would be recognized and so insisted on wearing a pair of dark glasses into the movie house. I was sure there was no chance at all of anybody recognizing him in this obscure theater and told him so. He reluctantly agreed to remove the sunglasses. Immediately, a man rushed over to him in the aisle and said, "Aren't you Paul Brunton, the author?" P.B. shot me a look of sad victory, and I learned my lesson, though I could not help wondering to myself, even then, if perhaps he had not orchestrated the incident precisely in order to demonstrate his correctness to me. I don't think he admired my budding skepticism when it appeared to turn in his direction.

During that same visit to Rome, P.B. went for a stroll with Linda and me one afternoon. Like most adolescents, I was easily embarrassed. P.B. spoke atrocious Italian, with an extremely marked English accent. (The same was true of his French.) He was speaking quite loudly, much to the amusement of some Italian onlookers, and Linda and I were acutely uncomfortable. He turned to us and said, "You are probably wondering why I speak such good Italian." Sort of, we nodded. "It is because in a former incarnation I was the secretary to the Black Pope." I did not know who the Black Pope was, but it sounded deliciously ominous and of enormous importance. I was young and resilient and would not allow anything to make a permanent dent in my devotion.

P.B. regarded any criticism as lack of loyalty. He felt free to talk about anything within the circle of our family, but he would go silent when faced with any question that even hinted at hostility. I may have entertained doubts, but never hostility. This made it fun for me, because I could ask anything I wanted. About death, for example. I once asked P.B. if he knew the date of his death.

He smiled. "It's already been fixed."

I thought so. "By whom?"

"The Overself."

I had heard about this Overself, a very slippery character. Sometimes P.B. called it The Mind Behind the Universe or even more mysteriously, The Mind Back of Things, or the World Idea, and sometimes just God. But his favorite term, I think because he invented it, was the Overself. The Overself was not up for discussion. It *was.* "You must have faith in the Overself, Jeff," he would tell me. "It will protect you, especially in difficult times."

"But where is the Overself?"

"It is your own innermost nature."

"But I can't feel anything inside like that. Are you sure?"

"Yes, I am sure. And you must have full faith in its presence and power."

"Will it help me?"

"Yes, but only if you have this full faith. It cannot help you without it. But with it, it will heal you when you are sick, and help you whenever you need its help. But you must pray to it every day." I found it hard to have "full faith" in something I could not see or feel, but P.B. was so certain, I did not dare doubt him. Besides, to doubt him was to doubt the Overself itself, a distinctly dangerous proposition.

Living with P.B. involved adhering to many rules, and hearing many legends about health, the body, and the advantages of living the kind of "clean" life we did. (I wondered why people who had no such rules often seemed so much healthier physically.) P.B., for example, had in his disdain for the body such elaborate rituals of what he could and could not eat that a good part of his day was spent trying to conform to these rules. I am reminded of George Orwell's comment about Gandhi: "It takes a lot of money to keep Gandhi in poverty." Attempting to avoid the needs of his body, P.B. seemed preoccupied with it to a degree rarely encountered elsewhere. Yet P.B. and my parents prided themselves on their lack of fanaticism when compared with some of their friends.

The one area in which P.B. made no concessions to other people was his vegetarianism. He was very strict about it. This strictness was not, as he frequently reminded us, merely on humanitarian grounds. He certainly treated animals with great gentleness and kindness, something I always liked about him. But he also felt that eating meat had a bad effect on the psychic aura, and that that made it more difficult to see truth. He considered "pure food" a qualification for the Quest; all of his disciples, as far as I know, were vegetarians. He once complained that Alan Watts ate pork, saying that such "gross" food creates impurities that impede spiritual progress. Smoking, too, was frowned upon. Still, I remember how angry everybody was at my reaction when P.B., as we were driving in Hawaii, pointed to a man who he said had attained a high degree of spirituality. I was about twelve, and I smugly said it was impossible, because he was smoking a cigarette. I was admonished by everyone at once, including my father, my mother, P.B., and my sister.

I was a terrible little prig about such matters, even at an early age. I recently found a letter my sister Linda and I had written to P.B. in 1954 from the Edgewater Hotel in Waikiki. My parents' trip to

Europe, just before this visit to Hawaii, had "changed" them in ways that Linda and I found distressing. They were slipping from the path. Eating meat was the most visible sign of this descent. We wrote:

Dear P.B.

It has happened. They're eating fish, like any other low developed cannibal. Could you please write to them and tell them to stop. For it is hard to live with a mother and father who are *meat eaters*.

Love: Jeff and Lin

I cannot help wondering how all of us—P.B. in particular—escaped being labeled mentally ill. While I reject the label, people who ferociously believe that they are in close touch with beings from other planets are, as we know, often locked up in psychiatric wards. Perhaps this was one of the reasons for all the secrecy in our house. For whatever reason, P.B. and our family completely escaped such a fate, and while P.B.'s behavior (fasting and meditating and searching out yogis) might well appear *odd* to many people, it was hardly as odd as what he *believed*.

It is equally odd *that* he was believed. I was a child, and I accepted what my family told me was true. My parents were disciples, and they accepted, for the most part, what their guru told them. Actually, my parents were slightly embarrassed by some of P.B.'s more outrageous claims, but they avoided any confrontation and have told me that they never even asked themselves point-blank whether they believed him or not.

Was it possible that P.B. himself did not believe what he said? I don't think so. His whole *life* was predicated on following what he said he believed. But if he believed such ideas, how did he maintain an equilibrium within a world predicated on wholly other ideas?

Chapter Five

Living with a Guru

I was fourteen years old and remarkably small for my age. I remember sitting next to a young girl I liked and finally summoning up the courage to ask her out on a date. She startled me by asking the question I feared most: "How tall are you?"

I lied: "Five feet."

I squirmed almost as much at her next question: "And how much do you weigh?"

I lied again: "Seventy pounds." She was considerably taller and heavier than I was. I was a boy, still a small child, and she was well on her way to womanhood. It was not that I was overcome with sexual desires at fourteen. I was not. But I definitely was interested in girls and wanted to be with them in some as-yet-undefined romantic way. My size was making this impossible. Nobody, in fact, could believe that I was fourteen. I looked more like ten.

And so I felt a certain bond with P.B. He too was small, almost as small and frail as I was. Yet he was an adult. And not just any adult, but the guru, the man to whom other, larger men deferred. I took my problem to P.B.

We were sitting in our garden, next to the pool at our house near Griffith Park in Los Angeles where we had recently moved. My tortoise was sunning itself in the rose bushes next to the water, my dog was sitting at my feet, and my cat was curled up in P.B.'s lap. It was a lazy Sunday afternoon, and I felt lucky to be able to talk for hours with the family guru. I loved it when he would sit quietly watching the little birds building their nests. This gave him intense pleasure. It was one of the few activities he seemed to enjoy for its own sake, without seeking to moralize about it or use it for some spiritual lesson. He just liked birds. So did I. "P.B., it's embarrassing," I said. "I'm so small. I'm tiny and my friends make fun of me. I feel like a midget."

"Jeff, I know about your problem, for I have it too. You see, people come to me after reading my books. You will notice that I don't put a photo of myself on the cover. This is because I don't want to put people off. They call me and want an interview, and sometimes I grant them one. At least a single meeting. I feel I owe that to my readers. But I feel like doing it less and less, even the single meeting, because the same thing always happens. They come to the door, I open it. They stare, dumbfounded. I can feel that they want to leave immediately; they think they have made some sort of mistake. The tone in my writing is strong, and they are expecting a powerful man to appear in the door. Tall, majestic, with long flowing hair. Instead they see me, P.B.: short, bald, thin. And then I ask them in: 'Come in,' I say, in a low soft voice, when they expect a trumpet to boom out of my mouth. And then I offer them a cup of tea and decline whatever they have brought me, and they are certain then that I am no guru."

"So P.B., do you feel bad the way I do then?"

"No, Jeff, actually I don't. And I'll tell you why. For one thing, I know that many authors share two traits I have: They are of small stature. Also they have short arms, just like I do." I had never noticed and could not see anything unusual about his arms. "H.G. Wells, who was far more talented than I am, for example, had short arms. Also, you see, you must remember that everybody has some physical shortcoming, something they are ashamed of. *Everybody*. Superficial people believe that when they meet the body of an adept, they have met the adept. The body may be insignificant in size, unattractive in appearance, frail in health. But the man inside is altogether other.

And if people like us, you and me, think about it, we can rise above the insults, because we can apply philosophy. We are, after all, philosophers, aren't we?"

Well, I was not entirely certain. I knew what P.B. meant by philosophy. It was not what I heard about in school, nor what I read about in the books I would seek out to learn more. P.B. was not referring to a subject taught in a university. A philosopher, for P.B., was no academic, but a person who thought in a certain way. He thought "philosophically." For me, this merely meant learning to think the way P.B. did. So I would apply his philosophy, his teaching, to all matters.

"Also," P.B. continued, "remember, Jeff, that I am not just an ordinary philosopher. I am a hermetic philosopher."

I did not know what a "hermetic philosopher" was. But it was clear to me what P.B. meant by the term: He meant that he was engaged in thoughts that others should not know about. It was secret. Being a philosopher was a little bit like being a secret agent. Other people were not supposed to know anything about P.B.'s life—not even his whereabouts or his identity. Especially if they were deemed to be hostile. He wanted to blend in, not to be noticed.

"I like to be inconspicuous in a crowd or when I am on the street," he told me. "That is why I dress so modestly. I could wear the robes of a philosopher (sometimes he did wear these "philosopher robes" around the house—a long flowing Chinese silk robe), but people would notice me then. I want to be ignored, for people to think I am insignificant"—he and I both smiled at the irony of it— P.B. insignificant!—"to be obscure, even anonymous. That way I can carry out my work without interference."

"P.B., what do you mean by interference? Do people really interfere with your work?"

Again the smile. How much, I thought, he would like to tell me, and how constrained he must be! It would be dangerous, I imagined, for me to know too much. Clearly he had deep and mysterious reasons for avoiding people. He usually shunned any physical contact, and I thought this might be connected to the danger he perceived in other people. I asked him about it.

"P.B., I notice that you don't like to touch people. When my parents introduce you to somebody new here in the house, you nod, or raise your hands in an Indian greeting of *Namaste*, but you never shake their hand. Is there a reason for this?"

"Yes. You see Jeff, everybody has an aura," P.B. explained, "a spiritual light that they give out. I perceive this, and I am very sensitive to it. I hate to shake anybody's hands, because I get contaminated by their aura. I need to preserve my psychic purity. If I touch somebody, the magnetic aura that surrounds his hands and body will mingle with mine. It is a kind of psychic contamination. I avoid it as much as possible, but it's not always possible. I feel ill when I touch somebody who is lowly evolved. That is why I often carry papers in my hands, so that I can have a good excuse for not shaking hands. I do not want my karma entangled with that of the other person. You pick up low thought-forms hovering in the other person's psychic aura, and they attach themselves to your own like crabs. You see, Jeff, the body is like a battery, and there are electrical radiations from certain parts, especially the eye. Through those radiations, a part of the aura is actually projected outward. This is why Indians of the higher caste do not like to have their food looked at by those of the very lowest caste. It is a polluting act."

"Is it something physical that happens?"

"Oh yes, you see, when you shake somebody's hand, it leaves an auric deposit on your own hand." I was fascinated. An auric deposit! What a strange and wonderful idea. Or was it?

"Should you avoid touching another person then?"

"Oh yes. I don't even like to be forced to sit in other people's auras. You know how I like libraries, but it is a problem there, because of the proximity. As you become more and more advanced on the Path, you have to be very careful where you sit, or with whom you associate. You should refrain from associating with anyone who is a failure, as you will pick up something of his bad karma." I wasn't sure what a failure was when applied to a person. But I was a little worried. How would I know when contamination was near?

"Can you actually see their auras?" I asked.

"Oh yes. Jeff, you remember what I taught you about the three different forces, don't you? *Everything* is susceptible to these three: tamas, rajas, and sattva. Tamas is dark, evil, low. Rajas is red, lively, restless, energetic. Sattva is pure, white, quiet, calm, the Good." I did remember. "Well, some auras are tamasic, they emanate an evil force. Each aura is a different color, depending on whether they are more tamasic, in which case they are darker, or sattvic, which means that the light will be very white. It is an indication of their spiritual progress, how far they have come on the path. When I see a dark light hovering over the head of some people, I avoid them. I don't want to touch them, or even talk to them. That is why you will sometimes see me slip out of a room when I see somebody approaching."

I had wondered about that. I could not understand why he would seem to be willing to meet some people he did not know, yet not others. I would be standing in a room talking with P.B., and we would look out the window and see my parents drive up to the house with guests. A man would get out of the car and start to walk up the stairs toward the house. P.B. would see him, gather up his things, and rush from the room, not to emerge until the person had left. Now I knew the reason for this. P.B. did not like his aura!

I remembered our earlier conversation about the people who wanted to interfere with P.B.'s work. For years, I had heard whispered accounts that usually stopped when I came near, as if the subject were too delicate or possibly risky to be discussed in the presence of a child. But I wanted to know more.

"P.B., is it true that lowly evolved people with black auras want to stop your teaching?"

"Well, yes, actually, it is true," he told me. "I cannot tell you everything, Jeff, because it could be dangerous for you, but I want you to know that there are certain adverse forces at work in the universe, forces that try to prevent people from discovering their true Self, who want to keep people from entering upon the Path. These adverse forces are very powerful. I have my own secret ways of combating them. I have been locked in deadly battle with them ever since I was in Tibet."

"Tibet?!" The word had almost magical connotations for me. Many of the more mysterious spiritual teachings (the so-called left-handed Tantrism, for example, that involved sexual practices—I heard it whispered about in the house) were said to have died out in India but were preserved in Tibetan monasteries. Many of the novels P.B. had suggested I read were set in remote monasteries in Tibet. But I had never heard that P.B. had visited Tibet. He talked a great deal about India, and the ashrams and the gurus he had met there, but never Tibet. Perhaps he had been waiting to reveal this secret to me. I was thrilled to hear it now.

The sun was beginning to set. It was one of those balmy evenings that still makes me love Southern California. All around me were homes where ordinary children were engaged in ordinary conversations. I thought this, and a shiver went through me as I realized how privileged I was to be in the presence of this great man who had learned secret teachings in Tibet.

I turned to P.B. and said, "I didn't know you had been to Tibet!"

"Yes, I try to keep it a secret. Actually I wrote a book, called *A Search in Secret Tibet*. You don't have to look surprised; you could not have seen the book. I never could publish it. You see, I met a highly advanced yogi there, a Tibetan lama of the Karmapa sect, a direct descendent of Tibet's great Yogi Milarespa. When the Communists found out that I had secret meetings with him, they wanted to interrogate me. I was warned before they came, and I was able to flee Tibet. But I was in such a hurry that I had to leave certain valuable manuscripts behind."

"But P.B., how did you talk to this lama?" I did not know if I would be happier to learn that he knew the mysterious language or that he communicated in some more basic fashion.

P.B. smiled enigmatically again, which led me to believe, of course, that both must be true, and that P.B. indeed did know the Tibetan language. I assumed, in fact, that he knew most of the languages of the earth. It startled me that his French and Italian were so bad, but I thought he must have been better with Oriental languages since India, I believed, was his true home. Actually, as I later learned, P.B. knew no Oriental language whatever. He derived all his knowledge from secondary and even tertiary sources. He did not outright lie, however. He would never say anything as crude as "I speak

Tibetan" or "I read Sanskrit." It would have been even cruder for a disciple to ask "Do you speak Tibetan?" or "Can you read Sanskrit?" The questions imply a degree of skepticism that was not permissible.

At the time, I did not suspect P.B. was inventing. Nevertheless, there was something about the way he described Tibet that sounded slightly unreal, some vague sense that he was simply amusing me, catering to my desire for the sensational. I am now convinced that P.B. never went to Tibet. If he had, I doubt he could have resisted the temptation to boast about it in his later books. Perhaps he glimpsed Tibet from Nepal; I am sure he spoke to any number of Tibetan refugees in India, and no doubt he had asked for and been granted interviews with various Tibetan monks and abbots.

But P.B. was not only attempting to keep me spiritually amused. It must have served his own psychic economy to think of himself as engaged in events that were earth-shattering, of the most urgent significance. It filled the same function for his disciples. And on his own psychic plane, in his own mind, P.B. probably did meet with this guru and many others. He identified closely with the Tibetan monks, who were persecuted and their monasteries razed by the rabidly anticlerical Communist government of China. It increased his self-importance to think that the Communists wanted him as well.

"Did the Communists ever find you?" I asked him.

"No, but they continue to seek me out," P.B. said. "They have followed me here to Hollywood, and that is another reason I must be so careful."

At the time, I believed it all. I was ever-vigilant when walking with P.B., looking out for the man with the Russian features who could be a KGB operative searching for P.B. to stop him from teaching The Truth. According to P.B., the Communists were just the outward manifestation of a much deeper hostile force at work in the universe. P.B. told me that he exposed himself to the attack of adverse forces almost incessantly. He had critically studied the ways of evil spirits, he said. "There is a psychological belt where millions of evil earth-bound spirits congregate and surround our planet. They become active at night. A human being can be infested astrally with psychic vermin."

It was a terrifying prospect. Would P.B. protect me from these psychic vermin? Was he protected? I asked him.

"Yes, I have a guardian angel," he told me.

This sounded Christian. I preferred it when he spoke of the "black depths of occult enmity" and the "harsh menaces of occult hatred" to which he had been subjected. I had been frightened but fascinated to hear him speak of the "Black Ones" and about "unseen malignant forces." This was absorbing; it intrigued my spirit of adventure.

"What do you mean by a guardian angel?" I asked.

"There is a higher power that is using me to write the books I write and also protects both my body and my mind."

Mind?

"Yes, you see, just about anybody else subjected to this kind of daily attack would lose his mind."

We had been talking for several hours. The sun had gone down. The birds were still. It was time to go into the house. P.B. had taken me into his confidence, and this made me feel proud, special, singled out. I was eager for our next conversation. While P.B. was always immensely busy, or so it seemed, he often made time for me. I thought I occupied a special place in his universe. I was learning things that would be important for me to know later, when I too would have to face some of the same challenges that P.B. had. The more I knew about his struggles, the better.

A few days later we took a walk together in Fern Dell, the park just below our house, wandering along the little stream with its small islands of exotic ferns and large overhead shade trees. There were rarely many people there, and P.B. enjoyed walking among the ferns and talking. I was hoping he would tell me about the attacks we had talked about earlier. I presumed they went on whenever P.B. left our home, for I never saw any signs of a struggle in the house. I asked him about this.

"Much happens at night, Jeff, when you and everyone else are asleep," he responded.

"Are you asleep too then?" I asked.

"Not really. You see, at night I wander through many lands, and a few are not even on earth. I travel."

I was a little puzzled. "With your body?"

"Not exactly," he said. "I travel with my astral body."

I was delighted and curious. The next night I set my alarm for two A.M., and when I woke up, I tiptoed out of my bedroom and quietly opened the door to P.B.'s room. He was in a chair, sitting straight, evidently absorbed in meditation. It was a position I was to see him in frequently. The next morning I told him this. "Yes, if you look in my room, you will think I am meditating, or quietly asleep in my bed. But I am actually traveling with my astral body."

"Astral body—what is that P.B.?"

"It is what the Hindus call the *sukshmasharira*, or the 'subtle body.' There is a magnetic field around our body, in which are stored all the thoughts and feelings from every incarnation we have ever had. This subtle body is not limited to time or space. It moves, in fact, much faster than the speed of light. It moves with the speed of thought. So you can actually visit any place you like simply by thinking about it."

"Can I do this too?" I was desperate to learn to do it.

"You cannot travel alone, but I might take you along with me one day, if your progress is satisfactory." I was afraid there was a catch. I didn't know precisely what he meant; no doubt it had something to do with physical and mental "purity."

"How did you learn to travel astrally?" I asked.

"My first teacher was an American painter, living in London. He was an advanced mystic, a gifted clairvoyant, an adept. He was a great occultist, brother M."

"Why did you call him brother M?"

Silence.

"I mean, what was his real name?"

"Thurston."

"What was his first name?"

Silence. I had learned that these silences did not, as I had at first feared, mean that P.B. was angry. He never was. It was simply his way of signaling to me that a topic was too delicate to discuss openly, or beyond my comprehension. It did not occur to me that he didn't know or, in some cases, simply forgot. P.B. liked a good story, though, and he always picked up the narrative: "He took me along with him on many of his travels."

"You mean to India and Tibet?"

P.B. smiled mysteriously. "No, places much farther away."

"You mean travels to other planets, to the stars, astral travels?"

"Yes. Actually, we spent a lot of our time together at the Astral University, where I studied philosophy."

Wow! U of A! Since I was still young, my mind was not flooded with all the practical problems: How did one apply? Grades? Who attends classes? Are there bathrooms? Where do the teachers come from? Was Buddha a professor there? Do they have faculty meetings? Degrees? Maybe this is where P.B. got his mysterious Ph.D. I don't think that as a child I was skeptical. I may, though, have wondered if he was just joking with me, but would I have dared to ask?

I wanted to know if P.B. was protected against what he spoke of as the "evil forces." Was this, I wondered, the function of the guardian angels? P.B. explained it to me.

"You see, Jeff, there is a race of invisible demons kept separate from us by a strong psychic wall. I am sorry to tell you that there are conditions under which they can breach this wall. This happens most during the hours of darkness."

I was already frightened of the dark, and what P.B. had just told me did not help. P.B. noticed his mistake.

"Of course, you should know that you always have a blessed presence at your side, and my power is greater than theirs. Mystic adepts helped me to exorcise these demons, and I can do the same for you. Should you ever feel a hostile force, open or disguised, immediately kneel, and then say very firmly: 'I command you in the name, by the power and compassion of Paul Brunton, to come out of my body.' Make a sign of the cross slowly with your right forefinger. Then inhale deeply and make the same sign, and this time repeat the same thing, but only to yourself, silently. No evil force can withstand this." (P.B. was not just comforting a frightened child. In his posthumously published book, *Essays on the Quest,* the same description appears.)

I was scared for a few days after that, and P.B. had me sleep with a green-colored light burning all night. This was something he recommended for all people, not just children, when there was "evidence of spirits." There was almost no spiritual superstition in which P.B. did not believe, but he bristled at the notion that there was anything unscientific about his beliefs.

By themselves, these conversations with P.B. probably did not make me feel any better—about being small, for example. But P.B. himself functioned a bit like an imaginary companion. I believed that he was a powerful, benevolent presence whose entire attention was focused on protecting me. My world was the ordinary world of a child. Instead of leaving me there to grow as a child, he took me into his world, with its bizarre suppositions and beliefs not shared by the world around us.

I thought that P.B. was describing the true nature of the world to me, a reality that was merely invisible. It did not occur to me until many years later that he was *creating* an imaginary world, though not for my benefit. He believed in it too. His words were like an adventure story of a spiritual Tin Tin, the French comic book hero; they certainly kept me alert and entertained. If I was not a direct player, at least I was important enough to be a recipient of information. I thought my role in this world would grow. I was young, but P.B. was still imparting knowledge to me that would help me when I grew up; that is, this knowledge would help me in helping the cause. The cause here was spiritual advancement for me personally and the ultimate triumph of spiritual values in the larger world outside of me.

It made the adventure even more exciting to think that it was also dangerous. P.B. liked to hint that those who opposed him would eventually come to a bad end. He often told me that it was not personal. He had nothing but goodwill toward his enemies, but the higher powers themselves were not so forgiving. It was, after all, he explained, the Law itself. By this he meant the law of cause and effect, or the law of karma. You get what you give. What goes around comes around. So P.B. explained that the Law would demand a hundredfold higher payment for every falsehood and every malicious word uttered against him. Forces were working for him—in the past, people had had to pay dearly for a hand raised against him. "And when the time comes," he told me ominously, "when the hour is ripe, they will strike again."

He explained it to me: "It is the worst kind of karma to insult a spiritually advanced person. It must be paid for sooner or later. Such a person will be struck down in time. If a man rises up against me, I will withdraw my love from him, right until his dying moment. I will appear to him in a vision then, and will forgive and comfort him. If you make a sage frown, there is grave danger." I vowed never to suffer such a fate.

It seemed only just to me at the time. After all, how could any person of goodwill possibly wish P.B. ill? But I suspect that it was not so much that anybody wished him ill as that not everybody believed what he said. The question of P.B. telling a lie had never even arisen. It was an unthinkable thought, although in later years it did occur to me that perhaps P.B. was not as innocent as he seemed. He was, after all, a journalist, with access to many people. He traveled around the world a great deal, visiting countries few people from the West went to in those days: Burma, Thailand, Malaysia, Ceylon. He sought out sages everywhere, traveling to remote areas. It is not impossible that some government agency, American or British, might have recruited him. He certainly would have relished the intrigue and the air of secrecy that working for them, in however humble a capacity, would entail. No doubt he could think that he was advancing the cause of spirituality by supporting the forces of democracy against communism or socialism. If he were working for the CIA, it would not have been paranoid to believe that the "adverse" forces were after him.

While working for P.B. in his little apartment, I had been witness to the many hours he spent in meditation. Several times I was allowed to sleep over. At night I would get up to go to the bathroom and often see a faint light coming from P.B.'s meditation room. I would tiptoe to the door and peek through the keyhole. There I often saw P.B. sitting on the floor, his legs crossed in the lotus position, lost in meditation. He was perfectly still. He had learned all the breathing and chanting techniques and applied them assiduously on a daily basis.

He spent at least two to three hours of every day in meditation. I find it entirely credible that he altered his body chemistry in some way, and I am sure this facilitated his withdrawal into another realm. Emerging from it, no doubt he felt that the experiences from within that world were as valid as those he had on this side. P.B. claimed never to dream. He told me that was why in just a few seconds of wakeful time he could have an entire night's sleep. He certainly did not seem to emerge from his bedroom with the tie to daily reality broken, as one might have expected had he really passed over into some other form of consciousness. P.B. was anything but "psychotic." He always knew what was real. But he chose, in some way, to ignore that reality in favor of another reality that he regarded as superior. When P.B. and his disciples used the term *psychic* reality, they did not use it in the psychological sense of "inner" reality. They meant a kind of higher reality, something from another plane, more rather than less real than this one.

Did P.B. ever have doubts or suspect that perhaps some of what he took for reality was nothing more than fantasy? I cannot imagine that he would never experience doubts. He spoke of such doubts often, though generally for others, attributing them to adverse forces. Any negative thoughts disciples had about themselves—about "the path," about gurus and their powers—were at best "tests" and at worst the work of external mischief-makers.

For P.B., the external world could not be *all* there was. After all, in this world P.B. was almost the opposite of who his disciples took him to be; he was hardly a force of any kind. He had no noticeable gifts; he knew he was less talented as a writer than many; he was unassuming in size and physical appearance; he had little money and no valuable possessions; in the eyes of this world, he had no power, counted for little. His friendships were not, by and large, spontaneous, based on a mutual attraction, but came from his supernatural claims. He had students more than friends. Although he maintained that he could teach in any university he wished, there were no offers to teach. Whenever he claimed to influence people in "higher" spheres, either the people in question were dead or he did not feel free to reveal their identity.

Perhaps it was to compensate for all of this that P.B. began methodically to create an alternative reality. In that alternative world, he was a man of immense significance. Perhaps, even, of unique significance. In his posthumously published *Notebooks*, he writes:

Buddha himself foresaw that a new teacher would arise within a few thousand years after himself, and that this man would have a higher spiritual status than himself. But what is of special interest is his further prediction that a higher spiritual path would, through this medium, be opened to mankind. Everything points to the fact that the date when this teacher and his teaching will appear is within the century.

Now, in fact, the "Buddha himself" never foresaw any such thing, according to any text I have read, and I have read a great many Buddhist texts in the original Sanskrit and Pali. I think that what P.B. was hinting at, or at least hoping, was that he might be that very teacher. He certainly thought that while Buddhism was fine, there was a "higher" teaching, the one he was revealing to mankind, learned in India from teachers now dead.

P.B. developed certain physical traits that somehow made up for what he regarded as his physical defects. He began to *look* the part of the Oriental sage. He worked hard, I believe, at cultivating a certain air of tranquillity that bespoke *inner* power. If he was going to be deprived of external power, he would have to have something in its place. People who displayed their power externally often behaved, in his eyes, like animals, that is, they expressed their emotions too freely. He would do the opposite. This was his primary complaint about women: "too emotional."

P.B. never exhibited any obvious emotion. Never would he express anger, become testy, or look bored. He would not yawn in public or give any sign of being under the influence of any feeling. Especially bad were what he called "the lower emotions." According to him, and from all external evidence, P.B. never felt a desire for revenge; he never felt anger; he never felt hatred. He did not appreciate the display of emotions in other people either. It came under the rubric "ego," the ultimate negative word in P.B.'s philosophy.

Almost everybody had "too much ego." Except P.B., of course. My father was fond of saying: "P.B. has no ego." What this meant is that P.B. never expressed desires for himself in the usual way. It is not that he never expressed desire—he just expressed it differently. Usually he expressed it with respect to the higher powers. Thus when he wanted a house, it was not for himself (this would have shown ego) but in order to carry on his work for others. He never took a trip for its own sake (he would never use the word *vacation*) but to perform some essential service to others, or to engage in mysterious research.

It is true that P.B. had few physical possessions, but the ones that he did have, he claimed had special powers. He had, for example, a small Tibetan statue. When I asked him what it was, he told me: "Three centuries ago there was created at the great monastery of Tashilumpo a gilded figure of the Grand Lama of Tibet. It was 'psychically magnetized' in his presence. Eventually it came down to the thirteenth Grand Lama at Lhasa. He gave it to a close personal friend, who then gave it to me." He kept it on his desk. "It is priceless," he told me, and I believed him. "Any museum would dearly love to own it." I was sure this was true. P.B. liked to think of his few possessions as "magic" objects, infused with spiritual power, although it is more likely that he picked them up in the Tibetan bazaar in Delhi. The little bronze statue of the Buddha I remember so well sitting on his desk was also a gift, from "His Holiness the aged Supreme Monk of Siam." It, too, was one of his personal treasures; it too was endowed with great power. What was important was the magic powers these objects possessed for P.B., and I think he considered them devoid of this power unless they had been in the hands of great sages.

Power was everywhere in P.B.'s world. What was this power that so obsessed P.B. and all his disciples, including me? It was something that would protect. It was like a magic wand. In fact, P.B. said that his own guru, the mysterious "brother M," always carried a magic wand. He said it was a glass rod, "potent with magic power." Could he have believed this, or was he simply trying to speak in the language of a little boy? I think he believed it, for his books refer over and over to just such childlike notions.

As for talent, while P.B. certainly did not have the illusion that he was a particularly gifted writer, he did like to hint that writers whom he greatly admired had some sort of secret relationship with him. When I was fifteen, I remember driving along the seashore outside of Cannes in the South of France, and we passed Somerset Maugham's villa there. P.B. asked if we had read *The Razor's Edge* and then said casually that the main character in this novel was based on him. Evidently, P.B. had met Maugham in Hollywood, years before and, seated next to him at dinner, had proceeded to tell him about his adventures in India. He was convinced that his life had so mesmerized Maugham that he had used him for the model of his novel, and the Indian guru, he said, was based on Ramanamaharshi. I was impressed and suggested that we all drop in on the writer and let him know who was passing by. My parents thought this was rather a good idea, but P.B. was adamantly opposed—no doubt with good reason.

He was certainly not adverse to meeting famous people. He spoke of meeting Charlie Chaplin and G. K. Chesterton, P. D. Ouspensky and Jiddu Krishnamurti, Rudolf Steiner, Karen Horney, and others. He told my family about a conversation he had had with Carl Jung in Küsnacht, in which Jung allegedly told him that he had to keep his mystical beliefs and experiences secret in order to guard his scientific reputation. He was very pleased at his friendship with the Queen Mother of Greece, who considered herself something of a disciple, or at least so P.B. always told us. Actually, my parents met her and her daughter many years later in Madras, and the meeting seemed to confirm that she had been close to P.B. Given her record of siding with the fascists during the Second World War, however, this would be little to brag about.

For somebody with no sexual needs, P.B. managed to marry many times. The marriage I knew best was to Eve, a striking opera singer who was then, and remains now, a disciple of P.B. He married her, he explained to me, for the sake of convenience (his; he needed a new secretary) and to help her spiritual progress. There was no sexuality involved, I was told. I was fourteen at the time, and just beginning to awaken sexually. I marveled at his self-control. I would gaze upon Eve, her fair skin, her bright red hair, her large breasts, and be seized with desire. I remember once when I was fifteen going up to the roof of a New York hotel with her to look at the stars. There we contemplated P.B.'s earlier existence. She held me as she looked up, and I could feel her breasts pressing against my back. I thought I would faint with desire, and I imagined that her breathing quickened too. She told me that P.B. did not need sex in the ordinary sense. "What about you," I thought, but did not dare ask. And in what sense *did* P.B. need it? I wanted it any way I could have it, and right then, with her, Eve. It was the most sinful thought a disciple could have. In India it is called *gurutalpaga*—soiling the bed of the guru, an ancient and much-written-about sin. Gurus who lived with their wives in the forest were often away and left their wives in the control of their young disciples. There was no greater wrong than a disciple sleeping with his guru's wife during his absence. I had read such stories and imagined I was in that forest, with Eve and P.B., barely able to contain myself, waiting for him to take his trip.

P.B.'s marriage to Eve came as a shock to many of his disciples. P.B. had declared so often that sex can only tear a person down, that a man is never satisfied, wanting constant change. It is dangerous, P.B. said, over and over, and should be avoided. All of this was well and good for the disciples, but the Master can make his own rules. Here is how P.B. explained his marriage to my father, recorded by my father in his diary:

"During the past ten days I met and was deeply impressed by the inner affinity with a young lady who was having trances and did not know how to control them. For a whole month around Christmas she was in the God-illumined state. Then she lost it. Now she has to regain it (which is her strongest life-desire) in the gradual way. She had a two year course of typewriting and journalism and wanted to help solve my secretarial problem, which has become intense and troublesome. Anyway, we decided to marry almost immediately in view of the pending trip abroad, previously arranged for the same week. I have no doubts about this marriage. It is God-guided and God-ordained. I do not need to marry at all, but the inner affinity is so striking, and the need to solve the problem of my work and to get help in attending to the many details of day-by-day living which absorb so much time that I need for more important matters has been an important factor in my decision."

It seems that P.B.'s marriage was a trial to many of his disciples for one reason or another. My father told me that when my mother cabled him the news in Japan, where he was on a business trip, he nearly had a nervous collapse. "All those years I had trouble with my sexual desire, and P.B. made it clear that I could expect no illumination unless I was abstinent. And now he marries!"

P.B. was fifty-four. Eve was nineteen.

On January 19, 1952, P.B. wrote a letter to Uncle Bernard, informing him that he had gotten married at the beginning of December and that his wife was accompanying him abroad. He said that the marriage was a surprise to him and to many other people as well. On the seventh of July 1952, he wrote again to say that while Eve had made great spiritual advances in the marriage, she wasn't able to keep her end of the bargain—to help him in his work. She wanted to help him, she simply lacked any capacity to do so.

P.B. never lost his sense of humor about the marriage. I remember him convulsing with laughter when he told my parents about the actual ceremony: Eve brought her mother along; the three were standing next to the minister when he turned to Eve's mother and asked: "Will you take this man as your lawfully wedded husband?" P.B. interrupted: "Excuse me, I am marrying the daughter, not the mother." The mother was his age; the daughter was young enough to be his daughter. P.B. thought this wildly funny; it never occurred to him that it could be construed very differently, as wrong.

My father could never bring himself to ask P.B. directly whether he was sleeping with Eve. This was, however, uppermost in his mind. A lot of the disciples wondered. No answer was ever forthcoming. It was not that it was nobody's business; quite the contrary, it was very much the business of the disciples, given P.B.'s stance on the matter. It was simply unthinkable that he would, and so nobody ever dared to ask if he did. P.B.'s description of it as a *marriage de convenance* certainly implied that no sexuality was involved. In fact, once the "convenience" was gone, once P.B. returned from abroad, he decided to divorce Eve. But within months, another trip came up, and P.B. married her a second time.

After the second marriage, Eve began to study voice at the Academy of Music in Santa Barbara. Accompanying her on the piano was a young, handsome, and gentle musician, Beau Regard Glass, who had been Lotte Lehman's accompanist. He was struck, he said, by her flaming red hair, white skin, and beautiful voice. He fell in love. She reciprocated the feelings, but was torn between the two men, her guru and husband, and the man she was in love with. Beau complicated matters further by asking her to marry him. She didn't know what to do.

One evening in 1957, when we were living in Hollywood, we invited Beau, Eve, and P.B. to dinner. The five adults and my sister and I were sitting around the table. At some point, Beau tried to reach Eve's foot with his, but by mistake he connected with P.B. Turning to Beau, P.B. said with exaggerated politeness: "Excuse me, you're playing footsie with the wrong foot." Eve blushed. Beau merely hung his head, forlorn. The rest of us burst out laughing, with P.B. laughing the loudest. Eve began to cry and ran from the room. But P.B. was in fine humor. He liked Beau enormously, as we all did, and thought it was the perfect match. He divorced Eve to allow them to marry each other, which they did within months, with his blessings. Beau now became a disciple as well, and both of them and their daughter, Melody, are fiercely loyal disciples of P.B. to this day.

I could never quite understand why I heard so much about sexual abstinence even at a young age. Did P.B. and my parents think that I should be caught early, before bad sexual habits began to build up? Was it part of my spiritual grooming? Abstinence continued to be held up to my parents as the ultimate goal to aim for, even if for a time they had to continue to be sexually active. After all, P.B. told them, as he told me, "Sooner or later, sex has to be given up." He was of the opinion that people in their forties no longer required sex. He may have been projecting his own needs, or lack of them, onto others. Or he may simply have been parroting the Indian tradition, which discourages sexuality, even in marriage, after forty.

One of the basic ideas of Vedanta is that "you" are not the body. A corollary is that other attributes of the body do not apply to "you." Thus the disciple is constantly encouraged to "rise above" petty distinctions based on physical needs or characteristics. But for some peculiar reason, my parents seemed obsessed with physical attractiveness: who had it, and even more important, who was lacking it. P.B. did not discourage this. For one thing, he was himself preoccupied with what he considered his own unprepossessing appearance. But even more important, he believed that "the condition of a single organ or of a half-centimeter of gland may curse a man's whole life more than any sorcerer can. The shape of his nose may be so disliked by others that his ambitions are thwarted or his desire for love defeated."

P.B. chose to deal with the problems of physical appearance not by transcending the prejudice through philosophic reasoning, which one might have expected. No, he thought it better to confront the problem surgically. And so at some unspecified time, P.B. had a nose job. So did my parents, both of them. I was fifteen or sixteen at the time and was urged to follow suit, but refused. Did my family do this for aesthetic reasons? Everybody had looked fine to me before. If anything, their earlier appearance had greater character and distinction. Did they wish to hide the fact that they were Jewish? I think so, in part.

It was strange, this bias against being Jewish. I really don't know if my parents adopted it from P.B. or from the culture around them. Being *too* Jewish for them meant that they were like the rest of their family, telling loud and crude jokes, or even worse, making fun of Eastern spirituality, hence P.B. But with all the emphasis on "the Truth" it seems odd that they should alter their appearance to hide the facts. Did they think it would help an unspecified sinus condition, as they said? I think that once P.B. lifted the sanctions on such an act, it was almost a prescription: If the guru wanted to change his appearance, surely we could and should. In many respects it had the opposite effect from what was intended. Instead of taking the family away from such trivial concerns as the appearance of the human body, it seemed to ground them more firmly in such a concern.

They were now part of the elect, or at least they looked that way, as the photos in this book demonstrate. Moreover, it seemed to them, at least, that it opened certain societal doors that had been previously closed to them. The effect on me was not so positive. To a certain extent, I was now odd man out. I didn't quite fit the picture of the perfect-looking family. I don't know how I resisted the familial pressure to change my looks and with it the appearance of my heritage, but I am glad I did.

The very idea of being a disciple of P.B. was fraught with difficulties and contradictions. He hinted, often, that he had no disciples, the assumption being that nobody was good enough to really be his disciple. On the other hand, in moments of intimacy he would tell my father and me that we were his disciples. This was invariably followed by a list of who was *not* his disciple. Envy among the disciples was chronic and deep, especially between my uncle Bernard and my father Jacques. Each wished to consider himself P.B.'s special disciple; I believe that P.B. told each in turn that he, and only he, was that person. He seemed to have something of a preference for my father, perhaps because my father was wealthier and able to provide P.B. with more comforts. Bernard was more cantankerous and altogether less reliable. My mother, being a mere woman, in his reflexively sexist cosmology, was often asked not to participate in the daily meditation, and sometimes was permitted to meditate only for a short period and then asked to retire.

Had P.B. been a complete fraud, at least one motive would have been financial enrichment. P.B. did not enrich himself at the expense of his disciples in the way, say, that Rajneesh later did. On the other hand, he was certainly not beyond taking a gift, even a substantial one. To some extent he justified this by citing the common Indian practice of giving the guru a token of gratitude. In ancient India this almost always involved fruit. A guru was not supposed to be paid—a worthy tradition around which ways had to be found. The disciple, many gurus say, must not be frustrated in his attempt to demonstrate his love for the truth, represented on earth by the person of the guru. My father's business evidently did not displease P.B.'s more practical side, for it meant that there would always be a steady supply of funds. Once, when my father was visiting P.B. in Mysore, India, he told him that he was inclined to cancel a trip he had scheduled to buy some gems in Sri Lanka in order to be able to spend more time with his guru. P.B. rapidly quashed the idea, saying to my father, "Your business is very important, and should never be neglected." Whenever my father made a large sum of money, he would send some to P.B. Sometimes P.B. would accept; other times he would not. It did not seem to depend on the amount. On May 28, 1946, for example, my father sent P.B. five thousand dollars, a large amount of money in those days, which P.B. accepted, though a bit later he returned a check for a much larger amount.

Over the years my father gave P.B. probably a hundred thousand dollars. Nor was it infrequent that a disciple would rent a home for him, in the desert, say, or by the sea. He always got the room he wanted, wherever we were staying, the one with the most spiritual (that is, the best) view. Once when I returned home from summer camp, I found that P.B. had been given my room, and I remember feeling very sorry for myself and not at all blessed or gracious.

Chapter Six

A Spiritual Boy in a
Swiss Village

In 1955, when I was fifteen and my sister Linda was twelve, my parents decided we should go to school in French-speaking Switzerland. This was partly so that we could learn French and partly because they felt life in Los Angeles was too provincial. The year before, P.B. had told my father, "You have a rare soul in Jeffrey. He will go far. He is well beloved all around. He can easily become a leader." My parents were trying to find the right environment that would help me "further my destiny." They could not believe that anything happened by chance or was done for reasons of less than cosmic significance. They believed P.B. when he told them that I was destined to become a spiritual leader.

So our whole family left in June for New York; from there we would sail to London, spend the summer touring Europe by car, and in late August my parents would leave my sister and me in Switzerland. As ever, preoccupied with my spiritual life, I was concerned that I found it difficult to meditate in New York, as well as on the ship and in London. I wrote to P.B. to tell him this. He wrote back saying that I should get used to the fact that "the results of meditation are changeable and that often there are no apparent results at all. At an advanced stage these changes disappear and it will be possible to go quickly and directly to the blessed state of beautiful peace within. Wouldn't you like that?" he asked. Indeed, I longed for these "advanced" stages of meditation. I did not want to be a beginner forever.

P.B. also told me that he hoped I would be able to become friends with "one or two nice Hindu youngsters of the vegetarian, spiritually minded kind." I was fortunate in my good karma and ought to make the most and best of it. I was destined to help many other people, P.B. explained.

We enrolled in a school called La Villan in a tiny village near Villars, about a two-hour train ride from Montreux on the eastern tip of Lake Geneva, not that far from the French and Italian borders and across the mountain from Gstaad. I felt as if we were entering a bewildering fairy land as Linda and I rode the little red Swiss mountain train from the plains up to the village. This was really our first time away from home, and a very close and somewhat insular home at that. To be leaving the United States, leaving our parents, climbing these alpine mountains for the first time was a strange and disconcerting experience. I wondered if Linda felt the same.

The village was very small (so small it did not have a name), quiet, and rural, especially compared with the larger and more cosmopolitan Villars. My parents chose La Villan because it was coeducational and Linda and I could be together. Also, it was a tiny school, with only some fifteen students, in a large Swiss chalet, and the owners had agreed to accommodate our strict vegetarian diet. Surprisingly, Linda and I adjusted rather quickly and well to this very different environment. French was my first spoken foreign language and I took great pleasure in it. Nevertheless, we both thought of ourselves first and foremost as disciples of P.B. and seekers of a higher truth. Rereading my diaries from the time, I am struck by how young and insulated I was, lost in my spiritual preoccupations.

Special announcement! P.B. was so right when he said my progress would slow up soon. I find it hard to meditate now, and so I'm taking the opportunity to build up my character which is improving considerably. I hate the talks with MacKibbin, the English teacher, as he is always tearing down my beliefs. It is, though, a good test.

Today we couldn't go skating or skiing, cause it rained all night. Everyone went to the movies so I got in bed early, read, and had my first good meditation since I've been here. Linda came up and we talked. She is very unhappy here, and I had to stop her from writing a letter to Mom and Dad asking to leave school. She misses Mom and Dad terribly. But I've explained to her that we don't want to spoil their trip, and she understands. She is a good girl and very spiritually minded.

It is hard for me to understand how I could have been such a pedant and prude, combining ignorance with arrogance and not have *somebody* tell me about it:

We went skating today at the Palace. At night, Linda called me in on a discussion on religion. They were all yelling and arguing and as soon as I spoke they all shushed each other and listened. It was difficult to explain myself in French, but I found that Tin a Ling who is from Thailand, is on the Path, and Mademoiselle Franco almost. We are going to continue Saturday. It was wonderful to find people so interested in the Path.

Or:

When I was young [I was all of fifteen at the time!] I lived in a world of good and right where every man was consciously seeking God and where pleasures were those pure ones that today I can scarcely picture in my imagination.

Or:

How happy I will be when I shall be settled down, able to take solitary walks, meditate, study, with no interruptions. Where I will be able to crush worldly thoughts, petty desires, etc., and in their place lead a life of serious, but oh how joyous, contemplation.

Linda was three years younger than I. Like many sisters growing up with an older brother, she wanted to be included in the more grown-up things that I did. So she hung out with me. Generally I was good-natured about this. She and I were close and shared many of our thoughts. Naturally, therefore, she tried to be like me when it came to spirituality and P.B.

But P.B., while fond of Linda, was not inclined to give much importance to women on "the Path." He thought that modern man had left religious faith and mystical practice to women, which was a serious mistake, since a woman, in his view, could never rise to the mystic heights that a man could. He considered women's intelligence negligible. Faith and mysticism had to be reclaimed from women. Perhaps because women were considered too "emotional," he tried to distance himself from emotions. He was afraid of being thought "effeminate." So Linda and my mother were both somewhat neglected. Linda twice, once for being a woman and again for being young.

It is hard to separate this from the fact that Linda was not as absorbed and obsessed with mysticism as I was as a child. She was altogether more skeptical, more practical, and less easily taken in. She never developed the "transference" I had to P.B. or the intensity of my connection with him. She did not, however, wish to be excluded entirely, and so she went through bouts of trying to become more of a part of P.B.'s circle of disciples.

Before coming to Switzerland she had asked P.B. to suggest some reading for her. P.B. told her to read *Brother of the Third Degree*, a trashy romantic mystical novel of which P.B. was particularly fond. I remember walking along the little alpine path behind our school one day when I saw Linda walking toward me, looking rather peculiar. She was gazing down at the ground and was taking very deliberate steps, as if she were lost in deep thought. I was intrigued and asked her what was going on. She continued to walk on in silence and did not answer me.

I was puzzled. "Linda, Linda, it's me, Jeffi," I said.

Silence.

"Linda, what's going on?"

"Don't talk to me. I have just read the first chapter of *Brother of the Third Degree*."

I went into a rage of indignation and would gladly have burned the disgusting tome that could produce such a pompous reply from my good-natured sister, who had never before been pompous. Moreover, she was attempting to usurp my role of spiritual prodigy. I realize now she was just trying to join the group. It is easy enough to say as an adult that that particular group was not worth joining. For most children, there is no such thing as a group from which you are excluded that is not worth joining.

We were there for one year when the school moved into a larger and less personal building in the village of Chesières-sur-Ollon. In the fall of 1956 our parents decided to move to Europe. They arrived in Paris in November, and after a month decided to rent a place in Geneva, where my father would be able to pursue his gem business, and where they would be able to visit us in school. My sister and I took the train together and met them there. That day I wrote in my diary:

Today was one of my happiest days I've ever had. We found an apartment today, what luck, or rather, what destiny! We had a marvelous dinner. It is wonderful to be together again and now that we are together again I realize how lucky we are and I thank God for everything. I never before realized how good Mom and Dad have been to us, how mean I've been to them by being cranky, etc. It shall never happen again.

I had my first real girlfriend in school. She was not the least bit interested in spiritual matters. One evening a hypnotist came to our school for a performance. He spoke melodramatically of unleashing dark forces into the room, and she became frightened. I told her she shouldn't worry, because I could unleash white forces of my own that would counter his forces. She was much impressed, but I felt I had taken a first step on the path to charlatanism. I was so scared at my own lying that I wondered at the time what I could have meant that was *true* behind the obvious lie. I decided I had meant that I would call upon P.B. and *he* would unleash the white force. P.B. liked to talk of white magic as opposed to black magic, and to hint that he could call upon it, *if forced*. On the one hand, he and my parents mocked and ridiculed the belief in what the Indians call *siddhis*, magic powers. It was considered a lower stage of development to want these powers. On the other hand, it was always assumed that P.B. had them but simply chose not to use them. To demonstrate them would have been a case of *lèse majesté*, and to ask him to do so would have been an unpardonable breach of manners. I was eventually to be guilty of this under momentous circumstances.

For a Christmas present that year, my father asked me how I would like to go with him for some months to India on a spiritual quest. I was delighted. While we were away, my mother would rent a chalet next door to the school. Now I wonder if they weren't having problems in their marriage. P.B. had told my father that a two-year period of sexual abstinence would be good for his spiritual progress. So there had been no sex between my parents for a long time, or so they told me. I think one of their reasons for telling me about this was their hope of retarding my own sexual initiation. My father was convinced that his side of the family, at least, was "oversexed," as he put it, and this had disturbed his spiritual advancement. He did not wish me to fall prey to the same difficulty.

My mother took a house with a young German woman named Doris, whom everybody despised because of her blatant anti-Semitism. I don't think she knew my mother was Jewish. The two beautiful women visibly flirted with the ski instructors in town. Linda tells me that she was horribly embarrassed and refused to visit our mother, even though she lived right across the street from the school. She remembers seeing her and Doris walking down the street arm in arm with two young Swiss ski instructors. She felt my mother was immoral.

I knew nothing of this. For me, the trip to India had nothing to do with my parents' marriage; it had only to do with my father's urgent desire to meet sages. Years before, he had dreamed of meeting the Maharshi, the Indian guru P.B. had made famous in the West. But his dream had been shattered in April 1950, when P.B. wrote to tell him the Maharshi had died that weekend. My father had often told P.B. how much he had wanted to meet the Maharshi. P.B. had always suggested waiting. Now it was too late, and I think the trip to India with me may have been suggested by P.B. as a compensation. To this day, neither my uncle Bernard nor my father can find it in themselves to forgive P.B. for preventing them from meeting the Maharshi.

P.B. was not uncomfortable with my father's desire to meet the very sages that P.B. himself had met while in India. Spiritual pilgrimages had a long and venerable history and were not regarded as a sign of disloyalty. For my father, however, I think there was still some vague hope that he would meet a guru who would instantly give him the mystic experience for which he had been hoping in vain from P.B. My father read about the spiritual experiences of others the way a bedridden invalid reads about travel adventures. Why could he not experience such wonders?

He was especially intrigued by the Indian notion of the kundalini, which he had already encountered with P.B. on his first trip to India in 1945. The kundalini is a so-called serpent-power, a reserve of energy, coiled at the bottom of the spine. Certain exercises "awaken," or arouse, the kundalini, which travels up the spinal canal through various centers of consciousness, called chakras, (circles), until it reaches the "highest" or seventh chakra, imagined to be somewhere in the brain, at which point a massive illumination is supposed to take place. Along the way, especially in the three lowest chakras, the trip produces certain extrasensory abilities. P.B. chided my father for searching for these "magic powers" so assiduously. But my father countered that they would serve merely to persuade him that the kundalini had in fact been awakened. Meditation was the primary means of arousing this beast, and my father had practiced it faithfully every day for more than ten years, with no result.

I was always a bit struck by how honestly my father reported to P.B. his *lack* of progress, without ever seeming to feel defeat or losing any faith in P.B. My father always told me that he did not believe these things were unreal, only that he was not worthy of them. He always blamed himself. Still, he had the not-so-secret hope that the right guru would remove the obstacles that had been preventing him from discovering the truth and thus gain for him access to all of these wonders, especially magic powers. He would, of course, put these powers to purely spiritual use, for the benefit of mankind. But he was eager to experience them directly, and soon. Time was marching on. For all the years he had been meditating, he had, as he put it, "nothing to show for it." A miracle, or at least a sign of some kind, was due.

My father also felt that it was time for me to visit India. I had been a faithful son, having ingested all the spiritual ideas I was fed by my parents and P.B. In truth, I was both emotionally and intellectually immature, suffering from a kind of spiritually created retardation. I had almost no sense of a real world: My knowledge of politics was zero; my awareness of the situation in Europe where I was living was nonexistent; my knowledge that other people did not live the privileged life that my family and I lived was nil. It was not that I was without empathy; I simply knew nothing of a real world of suffering, unhappiness, and especially social injustice (even the concept was unknown to me) to which empathy could attach. If ignorance is a sin, I was a terrible sinner. I was kept from the real world as effectively as the Buddha had been before his enlightenment. But I cannot merely blame other people. The world was there for me to look at, but instead I focused on an inward vision of a spiritual Shangri-La and buried my nose in my mystic books—a 1956 list I made of the five books I would have taken with me to a desert island included the *Bhagavadgita*, the Bible, the Upanishads, the Buddhist Bible, and the Encyclopedia Brill, whatever that is.

I think my parents saw me as a kind of Jiddu Krishnamurti, "destined" to play a leading role in the spiritual life of mankind. I knew the stories of the young Krishnamurti, how he had been

groomed for years by Annie Besant and the leaders of the Theosophical movement to become the World Leader they were waiting for.
The material and emotional perks that came with this, including
being the object of adoration of thousands of people, were considerable. It had taken courage for Krishnamurti to renounce it all, as he
eventually did, proclaiming, "Truth is a pathless land." He was no
teacher. He accepted no disciples. Or so he said.

Before the visit to India, we had visited Krishnamurti in Gstaad
for a few hours. P.B. was, again, the facilitator. Krishnamurti was
living in a luxurious Villa lent to him by—a friend? Not really, she
was a follower, a disciple actually, though she would not have called
herself that. If the land of Truth was pathless, some apparently knew
their way around better than others. Krishnamurti allowed himself to
be seen by others as a *guide*—which in the end was just a variation on
the guru theme.

Krishnamurti was a wonderful man to spend an hour with,
however. Handsome, charming, humorous, witty, he had "charisma,"
a quality P.B. lacked. P.B. had turned this lack into a virtue—it
somehow gave authenticity to his teaching. But they shared some of
their pretensions. Both pretended to know about matters in which
everybody is equally and profoundly ignorant—death, for example.
And while Krishnamurti rejected the teachings of his Indian background, he subtly and lucratively made himself an international
superguru largely by denying the validity of being a guru.

Around this time, I was slowly beginning to develop an interest in
girls. It felt like an outside influence, an external force imposing itself
on me. I was frightened that this interest would spoil my spiritual
progress—not an idea I developed entirely on my own. All my
spiritual reading reinforced it. An irresistible force, my growing
sexuality, was hitting up against an unmovable object, the years I had
spent as an aspirant to holiness.

My mother wrote to P.B. from Switzerland:

The children are quite content and well installed up in the
mountains. Jeff has a girl friend there, quite nice, but he says he

may not get married, though he'd love to have children. He says he's afraid of being diverted and have to re-incarnate once again. He's quite a fellow and growing up fast. Linda's a real beauty, and sometimes feels inadequate in a house full of yogis, she says. But she's doing quite well for her 14 years I assured her.

My mother's mention of my reluctance to reincarnate once again refers to the goal of all Indian philosophy: *jivanmukta*, or living liberation. This is the state of being freed from the cycle of births and rebirths, to have no further need of reincarnation because the goal of existence, self-realization (as P.B. called it), has been achieved. That is what I was seeking, and I was afraid that love for a person of the opposite sex would hinder my progress. This fear had been instilled in me by reading about abstinence, by P.B.'s many comments, and by my parent's many reiterations of the same admonitions.

I seem to have tortured my girlfriend Sara, and my sister as well, with my spirituality. I found a pathetic letter from my sister, whom I was desperately attempting to turn into my disciple:

Baby Brother:

"If you can't be a well, be a bucket. If you can't be a bucket, be a rope. If you can't be a rope, be a pully. But never be a stone that the idling passer-by casts into the well to hear its waters splash."

After reading your letter I opened the *Book of Mirdad* by Michael Naimy. That was on the first page. How true it is Jeff and how sad it makes me. Perhaps this school year has shown us something we needed to learn. I've been swept up in a stream of superficial actions and will soon forget that which I am searching for. I need to be awakened—I need help. I love you, almost more than Mom and Dad because we have always been so close. Here we seem to lose that closeness. I fill my time with idleness—how well I know it. But I am so fixed in my ways I no longer have the will to struggle upward. Jeff, you know what it's like and only you can help me. "The soul has its own currency." It seems that mine is gossip, friends, parties, imitation happiness. These are only passing and I need to have that real happiness not just illusions. Jeff you are a seeker on the Path as well as my brother. You can help me. Why do you think I am depressed? Why do you think I want to get away? . . . Jeff, I'm glad you're awake, but wake me too!

I love you more than anything in this world, Linda

It is a touching and sad letter for a young teenage girl to have written her self-obsessed brother. She may have been three years younger, but she was emotionally much more mature than I was. She had been made to feel inferior to me when she ought to have felt infinitely superior.

Sara seemed equally devastated by my constant judgments. "Women, you are both caught up in maya, meditate," I would tell them both. A few days after Linda's letter, Sara wrote me telling me how my spirituality ("you are a giant of character") shamed her. I was "pure"; she had to be cleansed. She was not worthy of my love. What had I done to turn such lively girls into self-loathing disciples? Was I practicing to become a guru?

Growing up, I knew that P.B. considered sexuality to be the foil to spirituality. For my father, it was his demon, the recognition that he somehow could never be part of the world that P.B. represented. Sexual abstinence seemed to come easy to P.B. but was impossible for my father. He told me so often and talked to me about it even before I knew exactly what he was talking about. But as I entered my adolescence, I began to know from direct experience what he meant.

In the summer of 1956 our family rented a house in Cannes, on the French Riviera, Villa Santa Roseline, from June through September. I was fifteen, and P.B. was spending the summer with our family. We lived in the hills, just a few houses away from Picasso. It was a significant time for me: I learned to drive, I took long walks in the beautiful wooded hills, I swam and attempted (unsuccessfully) to sail, something my father loved to do. But it was most significant as the summer in which I first became aware of strong sexual feelings. I had had fleeting moments before this, but now I was in a constant state of sexual arousal. I never told P.B. this, but I assumed he knew. I assumed he knew everything, and I knew that he did not approve of sexual desire.

I spent most afternoons at the beach on the Croisette playing volleyball and soon became friendly with a group of slightly older French adolescents. One girl in particular struck my fancy. She was seventeen, the daughter of the sailing instructor. She had long blond hair and a beautiful, voluptuous body. I stared at her freckles for hours, filled with an infinite number of fantasies. One day she asked me to go out with her alone on a sailboat. She could sail; I could not. I was to go the next day. I was in an agony of indecision. What should I do? I wanted to kiss her, but I had not yet really kissed, and I knew, only vaguely, that I would never stop with a kiss. What would P.B. think if he knew, and of course, he must know. Would he despise me if I kissed her? Would he be proud of me if I resisted?

The next day we went on the boat, and sailed out about a quarter of a mile. Suddenly Daniella took off the top of her bathing suit and invited me to admire and kiss her nipples. I began to tremble with fear as much as with desire. Here had come my moment of truth. My test. I told her I could not.

"Why not?" she said reasonably. "You seem to like looking at me." She pointed to my erection.

I decided to tell her the truth. I began a long, more or less incomprehensible speech about P.B., not knowing the French for many a spiritual term, and obviously and painfully boring her thoroughly in the process. She put her top back on, turned the boat back toward shore, and deposited me on the beach with a less-than-friendly "adieu." I did not feel triumphant.

I was glad to be able to turn my attention to nonworldly matters, to Indian sages who never felt sexual desire, and to my trip to India, which was looming larger and larger in my mind.

Chapter Seven

In India in Search of Masters

I liked to think of advanced mystics holding special councils (as a result of reading Hermann Hesse's *The Glass Bead Game*, which in turn
was influenced by Buddhism and Indian philosophy), at which my
"spiritual education" was discussed in great detail by elder statesmen
of the spiritual world. But, of course, nobody other than my parents
and P.B. (and even he only to a minor extent) was the least bit interested in what I did in India. This was probably fortunate for me. Still,
if the trip to India was not carefully planned by a plenary session of
adepts, my father certainly intended it to be a spiritual quest. We
were not ordinary tourists; we were spiritual tourists; we were going
to meet sages. The list of those to see—the few people P.B. considered "realized" beings, Ramdas, Atmananda, and Aurobindo—was
provided by P.B., and so had his stamp of approval. The trip was not,
therefore, an act of disloyalty. P.B. had met all the same people years
before. We were simply following in his footsteps. My father sailed
on the SA *Asia* for Bombay, where, since I did not want to miss more
school than necessary, I met him by plane, in December 1956.

This was my first trip outside Europe and the United States and my first vision of a Third World country. I was not prepared in any way for the reality of India, for the poverty and human suffering that I glimpsed for the first time in my life from the window of the taxicab driving past some of the world's biggest and poorest slums. The only way I knew to deal with this sudden descent into the real world was to immerse myself even more in the shadow world of spirituality. The appalling poverty and disease I saw when I arrived in Bombay did not really exist. It was maya: an illusion. What you see is not what you get. What you see, the suffering you perceive around you, is unreal, a philosophic illusion ("the external world is merely an idea, and a not very good one at that") and therefore need not be attended to.

India was particularly well suited to the spiritual insularity I had developed. It, too, suffered, to some extent, from the same debility, so we were well matched. Indian philosophy had long ago solved the puzzle of human suffering by depriving it of its reality. The philosophers were constantly discoursing on a cosmic double standard: Suffering, misery, and unhappiness were defined as such only from the *lower* point of view. From the *higher* point of view, there was no difference between the wealthy man and the beggar. It was, needless to say, extremely convenient as a balm for any conscience that threatened to erupt when faced with the suffering all around. This powerful rationalizing phrase—with parallels in many other spiritual traditions—was invented by a privileged Brahmin class to distract from the poverty and misery created by this same class.

Gandhi once suggested that all the Jews of Europe commit joint suicide to shame Hitler. P.B. held similarly bizarre views. He believed (along with Jung) that Hitler was a mystic, a medium, though an evil one. P.B. was convinced that the Holocaust was a result of mankind's karma and that Hitler was just a punitive instrument in its hand. "The suffering the Holocaust brings to people," he said, "is really the reactions of their own near or remote deeds. They are visited by the consequences of their own making." It is a cold view, as well as a remote, privileged, inaccurate, and heinous one. Similarly, P.B. saw the physical starvation and privation that afflicts so many millions in Asia as deplorable, but he thought "the spiritual starvation or moral degeneration is a worse evil." This was to be my guide to India.

The first guru my father and I visited was a man by the name of Swami Ramdas, who lived in Ramnagar, near Khanhangad, in the South of India, between Madras and Bangalore. He was a traditional guru who stressed *bhaktiyoga*, the yoga of love and devotion, especially through chanting the one word *Ram*, which is the Hindi name for the mythological hero-deity, Rama. Ramdas lived in an ashram called Anandashram that was patterned after those of ancient India. About a hundred disciples lived in this ashram, where all life revolved around the movements of the guru. Swami Ramdas himself was most gentle. He spoke excellent English. A small and quiet man of about seventy, he seemed quite frail. I could see why P.B. would like him. He was neither pompous nor threatening.

We stayed about a week in the ashram. I was not struck with anything Ramdas said, but I liked the peaceful atmosphere. I also liked that every day people were fed in the large dining hall, people who had no connection with the ashram but had come or were passing through, or were hungry. The food was delicious, my first taste of good Indian vegetarian food. I learned with delight to eat with my hands. I found it frustrating, though, that talking was forbidden or at least not encouraged during meals. I would have loved to ask the various sadhus—Indian holy men who came there to eat—about their lives.

They were a diverse lot: Some were naked, in defiance of normal societal conventions; some had let their hair grow for many years without washing or cutting it; some looked crazed, some looked wise, some looked weary. I wondered about their personal stories. I am sure most of them did not speak English, though, and it never occurred to me that there was a language I could have learned, Hindi or Malayalam or some other contemporary Indian language. For me, the only language in India worth thinking about was Sanskrit.

At our first meeting, Ramdas told us, "The easiest method by which we can keep God-remembrance is repetition of His glorious Name. Be always cheerful, fearless, and free. The name *Ram* [God] has an intrinsic value of its own. Because of its soothing melody, it has a marvelous effect on the distracted mind. Of all words, the word *Ram* produces the most charming sound. No two letters linked together could, by their harmonious music, lull and bring peace to the mind as the letters in the word *Ram.*" *Mantrayoga*, this was called, chanting of the name of the Lord. It did not offer much to satisfy any intellectual craving to think about what one was doing. I was bored. So was my father.

We were given a small private cabin in which to stay, a rare privilege. But I found it hard to sleep: When I put my head on the firm pillow, I could hear an alarming rumbling going on inside the pillow. Clearly there were a lot of noisy insects moving about in the stuffing. Could they get out? It made me nervous. But something even more disagreeable was about to occur.

A few days after arriving at the ashram, we were summoned to Swami Ramdas's room. He was surrounded by a circle of disciples, in the center of which was a woman vigorously washing his bare feet. As Swami Ramdas went most places barefoot, his feet were definitely in need of washing. However, I don't think this was the purpose of this particular ritual. I noticed that instead of throwing the water out, it was being carefully saved in a special container. When the woman had thoroughly washed both his feet and collected a considerable amount of the filthy water, it was placed in a glass and with great fanfare handed to me. I was given to understand that my father and I were going to be granted the rare privilege of drinking the holy water from the holy feet! I turned to my father in panic and asked him in French, "*Que fais-je?*" What should I do?

"*Bois,*" he instructed me. Drink.

I did. Then it was passed to him. He ceremoniously poured it over his head, a gesture that was well received by the disciples, as it showed even greater devotion than drinking. I later asked him why he hadn't told me about this trick, and he explained that it could only be done once. I thought the ritual was ridiculous and unhygienic. I wanted to vomit.

Swami Ramdas stressed devotion in the traditional manner. His teaching was very simple: He taught us a series of mantras to chant as often as possible: *Om Sri Ram, jai Ram, jai jai Ram* ("Om Blessed Rama, victory to Rama") over and over. His disciples did so endlessly. I thought it was numbing. But he also taught me a Sanskrit verse that I memorized and loved to repeat often, simply because of the way it sounded when I recited it:

*Satsangatve nihsangatvam nihsangatve nirmohattvam
nirmohattve niscalatattvam niscalatattve jivanmukti*

(From being in the presence of the godly comes detachment; from detachment comes the lifting of illusions; from the lifting of illusions comes tranquillity; from tranquillity comes liberation in this life)

Being around Swami Ramdas, I sensed the comfort it could bring to believe that the only important thing in life was devotion to God or to the guru. He was a most lovable, gentle man. But his views were so simple that both my father and I could not help wondering: Why be devoted to such a simple man? I yearned for wisdom, my father for magic. Ramdas never made grandiose claims. "I am but the servant of God," he would say, as his name implied. He never claimed to be more than that. Yet the devotion he required, no matter how quietly, somehow seemed to demand that he be more.

Swami Ramdas was in complete contrast to the next guru we visited, who was as rough as Swami Ramdas was kind. P.B. had written to my father about him years before in a letter mostly about the "entirely secret principal mission" that had brought him to India. He said that in between he had taken advantage of meeting the very few remaining gurus of any worth left in this country and collecting some more material from untranslated and unpublished texts. He wrote that he had been to a jungle retreat where an entire community of nearly one hundred souls comprised into family units were living in mud huts miles from the nearest village and surrounded by wild jungle. The guru was an old man of over eighty who was sprightly and vigorous. The aim of this community was to achieve the prolongation of the body's life far in excess of the normal. The guru, called simply "the jungle-guru," told P.B. that his own guru had been three hundred years old when he passed away. Another feature is that they were trying to conquer sleep, and nobody was allowed to sleep for more than three hours, while the guru himself claimed not to sleep at all. Also, they sought perfect health of the body, the development of the powers of astro-projection, and so on. P.B. had there met a girl of seventeen who had not eaten for seven months, taking only a couple of cups of coffee or tea a day, and another girl who was twenty-six, a "saint" who did not eat or drink at all for a couple of years. It was a most improbable description, but it intrigued my father.

It was this jungle-guru whom my father and I went to visit. He too lived in South India, a long car ride from the nearest town or village, surrounded by several hundred disciples in what was a kind of semidesert wasteland. It was not clear how old he was. He looked remarkably vigorous. From our first interview, I felt he took a rather sharp dislike to me and I reciprocated. Whereas Ramdas had stressed devotion to chanting, this guru seemed exclusively interested in magic powers, of which he claimed to possess an immense number. I think I angered him by saying I would like to see him demonstrate them. He said testily that I would have to live there for many years before he would show me anything. I said I couldn't do that, as I was still in school. He thought this foolish and said something to the effect that it could be arranged for me to stay with him "for a long time," and he looked significantly at some hefty-looking disciples who were more or less guarding him. They looked fierce, and all were armed. I felt very uncomfortable. I was struck by the number of guns—old army rifles—that we saw lying about. When I asked what they were for, the guru told me ominously that I would soon see. By that point, I was really quite frightened, and my father and I were led off to the little room that had been prepared for us.

That night I discovered what the guns were for: We fell asleep around ten at night, when suddenly I heard gunfire. Convinced that I had so angered the guru that his disciples were now shooting at me, I leaped out of bed only to see somebody outside shooting his rifle in the air. I went back to bed, puzzled. At eleven, the same thing happened. And at twelve. And so on, at every hour of the night until the morning. The next day we found out what this meant: The guru did not sleep, at least so he said, and he wanted his disciples to achieve the same mastery. In order to make certain nobody fell asleep, guns were shot off every hour. It seemed more like a threat than a reminder.

We had our second interview: "Master," I said, not taking any chances with being perceived as impolite or skeptical, "do you ever sleep?"

"No," he replied. "I conquered sleep years ago. I have not slept for many years now."

"Not even a little bit, to rest at night?" I persisted.

"I just told you, not at all. I have not been asleep for more than seven years."

I noticed, however, that at night the door to his large private room was guarded by armed men. Who would dare to intrude upon him, especially to see if he was taking a little catnap?

"I am beyond ordinary needs," he boasted to me. "I do not require sleep or food, and I take only a small amount of water." He was large, even corpulent. I did not believe him. "Of course, I have never known sexual desire," he continued, with what definitely looked to me like a leer. I saw the faces of the women disciples nearby go blank. I felt something slightly threatening in everything he said, as if he were daring me to disagree with him. I was beginning to find the atmosphere unspeakably creepy. "I visit the entire world every night. I even go to other planets once a month." I did not need to ask how he got there—I already knew. "Come stay with me for a year, and I will teach you to do the same."

"I will think about it, Guruji." This was a polite epithet used frequently in India for any respected person. The *ji* added to any name simply made it an honorific (Gandhiji, and so on).

"You don't need to think about it, just do it."

When the interview ended and we were out of earshot, I quickly told my father that I wanted to leave this place. He didn't seem reluctant himself. Within a few hours we arranged a car to take us back to the nearest town. It was with real relief that we said good-bye to the "Jungle Ashram."

Soon we were on our way to Pondichéry, the former French colony, to see the famous Auroville Ashram, a utopian "spiritual city" run by the disciples of Aurobindo Ghose. Aurobindo Ghose, known in later life as Sri Aurobindo, had been an Indian nationalist leader and mystic philosopher who had studied in England and earned a degree from Cambridge. The British had imprisoned him for sedition, and while in prison he had had a series of mystic visions that took him away from politics and into yoga. He retired to Pondichéry where he wrote a series of impenetrable books about "supramental forces," especially *The Life Divine* and *The Synthesis of Yoga*. In 1926 he went into seclusion and named his spiritual consort (Shakti) as the new leader of his spiritual community, possibly the largest in modern India. She was a French woman of Egyptian decent, named Mira Richard, born in 1878, known simply as *La Mère*, the mother. She looked ancient to me (at the time she was just turning eighty), but she had told the disciples that she had conquered physical death and would not die. It was widely believed that she was immortal. Thousands of disciples lived in the ashram, which was very modern by Indian standards and included a well-known university, libraries, and hospitals.

Shortly after arriving, my father and I were granted an interview with one of the Mother's chief disciples, who immediately launched into an account of the financial difficulties experienced by the ashram and said that they needed one million dollars. My father asked him, as a joke, whether he would be willing to accept a check or did it need to be cash? The man's eyes lit up, he excused himself, and within minutes we were ushered into the exalted presence of the Divine Mother herself. We had an interview with her for about an hour, in French, but we were constantly interrupted by people asking her about the smallest details of everyday life on the compound: Did she know what had happened to the fifth wheelbarrow on the vegetable plot? She did. Had anybody found a pair of sandals? She had them. I was amazed at what a hold she had on everything that happened there. She seemed ancient and looked to me as if she were about to die right there on the spot. But her disciples all kept photos of her playing tennis and insisted she was immortal and in perfect health. (In fact, she has since died, but not until she was ninety-five, in 1973. Her disciples refused to call it death, however, and said she had simply changed planes.) She said she wanted us to meet a young American yogi who was one of her favorite disciples and arranged for us to meet him later that day. She also suggested that we return for the holy *darshan*—a "showing" or a silent meditation, in which she sat on a little platform and three or four thousand disciples sat in a kind of theater around her. This invitation was a great honor, due, no doubt, to the amazing power of my father's imagined checkbook.

Later that day, we met the American yogi. He had just graduated from Yale and was very good-looking, large and athletic. He invited us to come with him to the small island that had been given to him by the Mother, whose picture he wore around his neck. It was a beautiful little island, and he had built a charming small house on it. I asked him how he had come to have such faith in the Mother, and he explained it to me:

"I always ride my bicycle to this little fishing village, where I keep a small boat to take me to my island. After a few weeks, I noticed a very pretty woman who always came out of her house when I was parking my bike and looked quite brazenly at me. When I realized what she wanted, I was very aroused. One day I couldn't stand it any longer, and I threw my bike down and started walking toward her. She smiled and beckoned me into her house. I started to tremble with desire, and just at the moment I was about to enter her house, there was a crash of lightning, and my stiffening penis was directly hit. It was a miracle my penis survived the lightning attack. The pain was terrible, but I was unhurt. The next day, when I went to see the Mother, she gave me a small orange flower. I learned that this stood for sexual abstinence. So she knew what had happened to me! It was a miracle."

The Mother had given me the same orange flower. In fact, as I later learned, she routinely gave them to anyone under the age of fifty, and everybody was amazed at her prescience. I always wondered what happened to that American.

That evening, we joined thousands of her followers for the meditation with the Mother and the silent *darshan*. My father was given a chair next to her, and I was on the ground on her other side. She told me that I was going to have a mystic experience that night. When the meditation was over, she asked me if I had felt anything. The truth was that I had. I was beginning to feel sick.

Sure enough, by the time we returned to the little French hotel where we were staying, I had developed a fever. My fever got much worse during the night, and by the next morning it had not come down at all. That day, I wrote to the Mother:

Douce Mère:

Unfortunately I have come down with a fever, and thus being in bed, I will not be able to see you this afternoon as prearranged.

Last night I had no Mystical Experience, probably due to the fact that I was uncomfortable, not used to sitting on the ground for meditation.

I am extremely grateful at having had the blessed opportunity of talking with you. I cannot fully express my thanks for the Spiritual help I have received from you. It was certainly worth coming all the way from America for this alone.

I would appreciate it greatly if you could write some personal advice to me on the large photo of yourself, and anything you like on the remaining photo and book. I would consider this a great blessing.

I humbly prostrate myself at your blessed feet,

Jeff Masson

By the next night, my fever was over 105 and I had become delirious. My father was very worried, especially after an ashram doctor examined me and told him that there was "little hope"; my best chance was to pray to the Mother. I saw my father walk to the door with him and then burst into tears. For some reason I was not frightened. My father immediately arranged to see another doctor from town. He came and said he found my illness puzzling. He thought nothing could or should be done, but he did not think I would die. I felt a little better, but when I got up to go to the bathroom and reached to turn on the light, I fainted.

My father was terrified. The fever lasted on and on, day after day. Already very small and thin, I lost a considerable amount of weight, as I could take no food. Finally, after about fifteen days, the fever began to recede. But we still could not leave Pondichéry, as I could barely walk from weakness. So I stayed in the hotel room and my father brought me books to read: the twenty-one volumes of Aurobindo's collected works. They were turgid, unreadable mystic poems and spiritual prose. A typical passage:

> If I had been standing on the Supermind level and acting on the world by the instrumentation of Supermind, the world would have changed or would be changing much more rapidly and in a different fashion from what is happening now. My present effort is not to stand up on a high and distant Supermind level, but at the present stage the progressive supramentalisation of the Overmind is the first immediate preoccupation and a second is lightening of the heavy resistance of the Inconscient.

The other books were all about the Mother: "Reject immediately every feeling, every impulse that makes you draw back from the Mother." Or: "There is not much spiritual meaning in keeping open to the Mother if you withhold your surrender. . . . all has to be done by the working of the Mother's force aided by your aspiration, devotion and surrender." Unreadable, even depressing.

I hungered for something secular and prosaic. My father visited the French bookstore and brought me back Guy de Maupassant in French. That was much better, but I was most eager to leave the city and the ashram. I still think that I must have fallen ill from drinking the foot-water a few days earlier.

The next guru P.B. had recommended was to play a major role in my life for the next few years and in both my parents' lives for many years to come, the catalyst to dislodge P.B. His name was Krishnamenon, or Gurunathan, or Atmananda, and he lived in Trivandrum, in Kerala state. He taught a particularly severe and intellectual form of Advaita

Vedanta, the Hindu monistic philosophy of which the seventh-century Indian philosopher Shankaracharya was the main exponent. He had absolutely no tolerance for any form of devotion, for rituals, for any talk of any of the staples of Indian religion, karma, reincarnation, meditation. "Pure nonsense," he would declaim, "all of it."

It was exhilarating talking to him, though I found his teachings above my head. Still, seeing him galvanized a certain latent criticism of the kind of spirituality I had been ingesting from P.B. Remarkably, it seemed to have the same effect on my father. For one thing, Gurunathan represented a certain tradition that has always existed in India in which secrets, mystery, occult powers—in short, all the paraphernalia that usually surrounds a religious cult of whatever kind—is dismissed as intellectually dishonest, ignorant, and inimical to true spirituality. He did not pretend to possess any powers. He did not say that there were things he could not reveal now. He did not engage in any of P.B.'s manipulative maneuvers. He was completely straightforward: "I have a philosophical point of view [monism] that I want to get across to you. Here it is. Think about it."

Gurunathan was the author of two books, *Atma-Darshan* and *Atma-nirvriti* in English, which we both began to read with absorption. They are uncompromisingly intellectual—"pure Advaita Vedanta," as his disciples say. Here are some excerpts from *Atma-Darshan* (*At the Ultimate*), written in 1946:

> Water by itself can never form a wave. Likewise Consciousness by itself can never form a world.
>
> Therefore the world is not, has never been and is never going to be.
>
> What is really existing is Consciousness alone. Consciousness is Happiness itself. The Atma signified by the world "I" is also That.

Similarly, in *Atma-Nirvriti* (*Freedom and Felicity in the Self*) (1952), we read:

It is experience that must prove the existence of anything. An object as such is never experienced. It is the knowledge of it that may be said to have been experienced. Even this is not strictly correct. If an object is not experienced it must be held to be non-existent. How can there be knowledge of a non-existent thing? Therefore it is not even the knowledge of an object that is experienced but knowledge itself. Thus experience proves that the entire objective world is knowledge and knowledge alone. That is consciousness and that is ATMA.

In other words, trees in Indian forests make no sound if no one experiences them.

I can see why India was so congenial to P.B. When we had traveled together, he had always been delighted to discover a new vegetarian restaurant. He would immediately make a note, and it would always arouse his interest if I told him that I had seen a vegetarian restaurant somewhere. When I first arrived in India, while driving from the airport to Bombay in the taxi, I dutifully made a note of the first vegetarian restaurant I noticed, and then the second, and third, until I realized that there was not going to be any end of vegetarian restaurants in India. They were everywhere. In a similar manner, wherever my father and I went, we made a point of searching out gurus and their disciples. In India, this was like searching for a vegetarian restaurant: swamis, gurus, masters were everywhere.

While in Madras, we spent the day with somebody called the Chidambaran Swami, a man in his nineties who in his early twenties had met Ralph Waldo Emerson. (Emerson died in 1882.) In Calcutta we met a guru who was supposed to be two hundred years old. He looked three hundred. We met gurus who didn't eat, gurus who didn't sleep, gurus who didn't die, not to mention the more common theme of giving up sexuality, property, possessions, and family. These gurus were constantly trying to outshine one another when it came to renunciation, to giving up something desirable. It was especially common for a guru not to speak. Meher Baba had not spoken for forty years. When he finally did, what he said was so banal, some wished he had kept to his old ways.

In ancient India, sages were continuously making a vow to give something up permanently, from a particular food to all food; from saying certain things to saying anything. This was considered a particularly economical way to gain merit. Even more important, it was supposed to confer power. I think the psychology is that since most men—despite the Mother, almost all gurus were men—want wealth, companionship, sustenance, communication, and pleasure, *not* wanting them confers a kind of power. This power can be stored up, like money in a bank, where it grows and grows. The more you abandon, then, the more you acquire; what you acquire changes; *that* you acquire stays the same. You give up worldly power to achieve spiritual power, which then—paradoxically but purposefully—gives you worldly power. Not to want what other people want, including their forms of power, is to have power, and also to acquire power over *them*.

We also went to Sri Lanka, which was then still called Ceylon. We visited a number of Buddhist monks, primarily European ones, because these were the ones P.B. seemed to know. Neither of us were as taken with Buddhism as we had been with Hinduism, but the purpose of our trip there was not primarily spiritual. My father wanted to do business. Sri Lanka was the center of the world for blue star sapphires, star rubies, and cat's eyes, which had been his specialty for many years, along with pearls. I loved going with him to the various merchants and buying star sapphires. I soon learned what the desirable colors were and quickly got involved in the fun of bargaining. It was a very different world. The risks were considerable, since some of the stones cost as much as $50,000 in 1950 dollars. If my father made a mistake, he could be stuck with a very expensive loss.

I had my sixteenth birthday in Sri Lanka, four months after arriving in India. We were staying at the Mt. Lavinia Hotel on the beach outside of Colombo. As my father and I walked on the beach, we saw a man bring his working elephant down and bathe it in the ocean. Apart from the spirituality, the physical atmosphere of both

India and Sri Lanka had a profound impact on me. I liked the sounds
and the smells, the heat, the luscious tropical flora, giant fronds,
towering jasmine trees, the fruits I had never tasted before (*sitaphal*, a
kind of cherimoya). Large alligatorlike animals (a species of water
lizard) lazily walked across a downtown street in Colombo and went
swimming off in the three-foot-deep gutter. I was taking it all in in
ways that had nothing to do with spirituality. I decided I wanted to
return to Sri Lanka one day to learn Pali, the language of ancient
Buddhism. (I did so, in 1966.) I can remember the very dishonorable
and then unbearable thought that I would still feel attached to this
place even if I lost interest in spirituality.

We returned to Bombay, where I found a strange book in a spiritual
bookstore: *The Book of Mirdad* by Michael Naimy. He had been a close
friend of Kahlil Gibran, and the book is in a similar style to Gibran's
The Prophet. I wrote the author a letter that captures the spirit of my
own unbelievable naïveté better than any account I can give:

April 3, 1957

Dear Mr. Naimy:

I am a boy of 16 and have now been "interested" so to
speak for 3 years in the "quest" or the Divine side of life. Dr. Paul
Brunton, a well-known adept in this field, has been a close friend
of our family for many, many years. Before arriving in India, I
spent several days with him in Rome.

For the past 3 months now, my father (who has been
interested for 15 years) and I have been touring India in search
of Truth. True, all necessary may be found within us and guidance can come most assuredly from within, but as I often say to
my father, a bee in search of honey has no prejudices, or rather
realizes no differences. It collects nectar from all flowers which
contain it. We are somewhat the same. The truth is not reserved for one person, and whosoever shall have it, I am willing
to humbly prostrate myself before him and receive whatever

fragments I can assimilate, even if these people contain it to a lesser degree, I am willing to learn whatever possible.

I very greatly desire to attain self-realization in this life. My whole life shall be thus devoted to this end. . . .

In Swami Ramdas's Ashram, I chanced upon your book, the Book of Mirdad, which fascinated me from beginning to end. Much of what I was seeking I found contained within its pages. New horizons were revealed to me. Also, many of the older truths which I have been trying to comprehend were put in such a new and wonderful way that I could not help but re-read the book several times. This was 3 months ago. It is truly amazing how the unfolding process within one works. Each time I read your Divinely inspired book, more and more of it becomes clear to me. I often found it necessary to bring several of these thoughts into meditation to thoroughly assimilate them. . . .

Now I realize how little of its esoteric meaning I actually understood upon first reading. Many parts of it, to my surprise (please do not think me vain) resemble my own notes, which I write regularly whenever inspiration comes. The resemblance is most assuredly a direct result of the great influence your book has had on me. There are, however, several things which puzzle me in your book, such as the Trinity of being. So far as I interpret this, it represents the absolute, the individual ego-soul and the higher self, which shall certainly through duality return them to unity. Am I right?

The perfect balance also escaped my comprehension. In time, however, with spiritual maturity all shall be made clear to me. I am content to wait so long as there is no maya or ego or doubt to interfere with my progress. . . .

By a strange stroke of Faith, surely a karma guided one, I received your address and obtained some information on yourself from Tripathi, your Publishers in India. They showed me your letters and I thus learned of your whereabouts and, excuse my audacity, willingness to help a struggling soul.

I, in my impetuous manner, wanted to send you a telegram asking if it would be possible for me to stay several days with you and receive your teachings. The more I thought of this, the more I desired it, but for two distinct reasons we decided it unfeasible. First, and most important, to impose on you in such a manner is sheer audacity, lack of taste and utterly unheard of. Next, my mother and sister are waiting for us in Switzerland, where we shall return on the 4th April by plane. We stop at Damascus and Beyrouth, from where I thought I could meet you and in about a few days time return by plane to Switzerland where my sister and I are studying (for the last 2 years), but we ordinarily live in America. We intend, however, to go to South America next year, for fear of a future World War which seems pending. What may I ask is your opinion on this matter? Of course, being but a child, all forms of courtesy are unfortunately dropped for my own demands and thus being, I thought of staying with you. I fail to realize that my own excited manner and yearning for knowledge has made you seem to me quite close, as if I had known you for several years. This, however, I fail to realize is not equally felt by you—you have not even heard of me, and I expect too much. It may be possible, however, with your consent, for me to fly to meet you from France, where we will be for a few months before returning to America. I fully realize what a demand I am making on you, but I feel what a help it would be for me to receive your teachings.

In case you would like any references about me, you may, if you so desire, receive them from: Dr. Paul Brunton, Box 339, Times Square Station, New York 36, New York or Swami Ramdas, Anandashram, Via Khanhangad Station, South India.

It would most certainly be God's will if by some way I could meet you. At first thought this idea seemed absurd, now it is becoming a divine reality. Truly, if it is so possible, my karma must certainly be a good one. God's Grace is unlimitable and I am abashed at my own unworthiness. My every move seems guided towards a spiritual end, as are all moves.

Faithfully and devotedly yours,
Jeffrey Masson

The combination of brashness, naïveté, and sense of entitlement displayed in this letter were to remain with me for years. Michael Naimy and I never met, but we corresponded for the next five years. At one point, I had memorized his entire book.

Shortly after my sixteenth birthday, my father and I returned to Switzerland. My mother moved back to Geneva with him. Whatever problems they might have been having, the four-month separation seemed to have cured them. I went back to school. I became more spiritually minded than ever. I meditated longer, typed out spiritual sayings and pasted them on my wall, painted my ceiling black with little yellow stars so I could be reminded of infinity as I fell asleep, and in general was as much of a spiritual puritanical pest (though I was of course in a way merely attempting to please the adults who encouraged me) than ever. In one of my later letters to Naimy (April 29, 1957), I surely reach my pinnacle of spiritual obnoxia:

I am enclosing two photos; the colored one is of my sister, mother and myself, after Dad had left for India. Through begging and extensive persuasion I finally got to meet him in Bombay. The reason they let me go was that I convinced them that this year was an important one in my spiritual career and it was necessary I be among spiritual people. I was more right than I then realized. My mother, also a very earnest Seeker, had been to India the year before. She sacrificed herself to be with my sister. She now wants to atone for it and therefore wants to come and see you with me if I go. How long could we stay in Biskinta? In case these photographs do not serve your purpose [I imagined he would put them to some mystic test of authenticity], I can send you one of myself in meditation which I shall take in a few days, and can send to you in my next letter. How I wish I could have known you sooner and that I could have grown up in your company to share with you my aspirations and my heart. . . . I have been blessed to have been born in such a family. With both a father and mother far more advanced than I am to help me along. They send you their warmest greetings and humblest devotion.

I had this strictly linear sense of a spiritual path upon which I was walking, hoping to catch up with those further along and always seeking somebody who could guide me. I was looking for a shortcut, which has a venerable history in mysticism: Both Hinduism and Buddhism speak of the "short path" upon which one might have a "sudden illumination," thereby making the dreary trudge unnecessary. Like my father, I was waiting.

I was only in Switzerland for a few months. In the summer of 1957, my family went again to the South of France. This time P.B. was not able to join us. The four of us were there from June to August in the Villa Lou Mieou in the hills above Cannes. As usual, we sought ways to advance our spiritual progress, including by meeting the people we thought P.B. would want us to meet. We learned that Madame Alexandre David-Neel, who claimed to be the first European woman to have visited Tibet, dressed as an Indian monk, lived nearby in Digne. She was ninety-three. She had written a series of books, including the ever-popular *Magic and Mystery in Tibet*. P.B. had long admired her. He suggested we try to find her, and we did. She agreed to see us because we knew the Mother, whom she had known when they were both young in Paris, and she was curious about her.

We were ushered into an ancient, large villa that now resembled a Tibetan shrine. She asked about our trip to India. She told us that she had been born in Paris but had left when she was young for the Orient. She had spent thirty years in Tibet. She was quite amusing, telling us a series of improbable adventures, including that she conjured up an image of a monk to keep her company in her lonely mountain hut, only to find that the young fellow would not leave and became sexually obsessed with her. "It took me six months to materialize him and just as long to dematerialize him. He was very annoying," she told us. This sounded like a cover for a tryst, but she told the story with great gusto. She manifested a refreshing lack of piety. We spent most of the afternoon engaged in spiritual gossip, which P.B. would have enjoyed immensely. Suddenly, my mother asked her what she thought of the possibility of a third world war.

"There will be one, but I will not be here, since I intend to die this year," she said.

The war. It was to dominate our lives for years.

Chapter Eight

World War III

The first I remember of talk about an imminent Third World War was in 1956, when I was fifteen. But as early as 1947 my father had written in his diary:

> Palm Springs, February 17th. P.B. spoke about a new World War. He said that in 1942 he was told it would be in 20 years, meaning 1962. The whole world will be in it. No safe place in the world. It would be advisable to live in the country. However destruction might reach a radius of a 1000 miles. The best place to live for a person on the Path is a place like Palm Springs or in a quiet country atmosphere, away from city noise, turmoil, distraction, etc.

Evidently, P.B. had been predicting such a disaster for some time. In volume nine of his *Notebooks*, P.B. claimed that "during the First World War a few illumined seers knew how it would begin and end, and had already known that a second war would break out about twenty years later." These same people knew about the outcome of World War II, or at least they knew it by 1942. How did they know? P.B. said it was not through reasoning or calculation, but by "revelation."

Why was there going to be a Third World War? P.B. was a consummate moralist; he believed the world deserved a war. He often said that the First World War had come about because civilization was what he called "sex-ridden," and that the world had then "plunged more wildly than ever in the quest for sexual joy," bringing about the Second World War. P.B. believed that semen, the gift of life, was not to be wasted. This is a popular Hindu notion. As he reasoned in the *Notebooks*, since semen is white blood, "nature has punished man's careless dissipation of the one with a forced loss of the other." Because humanity had still not learned its lesson about sexual irresponsibility, we were about to be visited by "the horror of a third world war, compared with which the second will be mere child's play." He called it Armageddon. It would devastate five continents.

There was also a "higher purpose" to the war: to "guard the higher philosophy" of the Quest and "preserve the Quest's practices and disciplines." The Quest had been ignored by too many people. Those who could best serve P.B. were therefore singled out to survive. Their good karma was due precisely to the fact that they had devoted themselves to the Quest. Surviving the Third World War, devastating to everyone and everything else, was to be their reward.

But while P.B. had been hinting for years that a disaster, a nuclear holocaust, was about to engulf our planet, I think he first began speaking to us in detail about World War III in the late 1950s. The Third World War was due to begin sometime in 1961 or 1962. For many years prior, the lives of his disciples were taken up with planning for this momentous upheaval. P.B. was busy with his own "work," which included averting this disaster via consultations with the higher powers.

This involved incredibly complicated visits to many countries. P.B. was always traveling. As I read his letters, the enormous number of countries he visited every year is amazing. He went to Czechoslovakia, Denmark, Holland, Belgium, France, England, and Switzerland, year after year, on trips paid for by different disciples. How I longed to accompany him! The only one allowed was a secretary, however—his own wife, Evangeline. The rest of us were supposed to be busy not with averting nuclear war but with the more mundane task of finding a safe refuge. This involved a fair amount of "research" about where nuclear fallout was less likely or less dangerous. Linda and I were still in school in Switzerland, and my parents were living partly in Europe and partly in Los Angeles. P.B. stayed with them on and off, but mostly he was busy.

P.B., too, was involved in research, but of a more exalted kind. He was conferring with four higher beings—the Four Archangels who evidently lived on his home star of Sirius—to see what could be done to save planet Earth. The only hope, he told us, was "the intercessory and contributory meditations of a few knowledgeable sages." I always presumed that P.B. knew other "Sirians" whose iden- tity he could never reveal. But it turned out that he could not just ask one of the Four Archangels, or any of the superior beings from an- other planet, where to go to be safe. Evidently they told him that he, too, had to find out the hard way, just like the rest of us, by elaborate research connected with radiation fallout, wind direction, and so on.

P.B. claimed that one of his disciples worked for the Atomic En- ergy Commission. While none of us had ever met this man, it is pos- sible that P.B. did know somebody there. In any event, he started amassing mounds of literature and poring over maps of the different parts of the world that he thought would prove safe from the deadly emissions—there was much talk of strontium 90—that would be re- leased during a Third World War. The talk was less of the war itself than of the bombs that would be dropped and the ensuing fallout. Endless letters were written among the disciples about where the saf- est place on Earth would be. Meanwhile, a few "chosen" disciples were being warned to wind up their business affairs in the United States and flee for safer realms. Much thought and discussion was given to determining where those safer places were, even though P.B. often said that "the Higher Self will tell you where to go."

But the Higher Self needed help. P.B. said that he was in touch with a high official of the Kennedy administration who—in great se- crecy and with much risk—would furnish him with a clandestine map of the world on which the safest locations would be marked.

This map had to be obtained directly from Washington. Uncle Bernard was delegated to make a special trip there to obtain it. Bernard flew, dressed so that nobody could recognize him (as if anybody knew him anyway), and was met at the airport by a mysterious-looking stranger who, after much looking about and furtive changing of locations, handed over a small packet and immediately fled. Bernard opened the package to find a map of the world with a small mark next to Uruguay and Ecuador. He was later to complain with some bitterness that the map was one anybody could have purchased in Woolworth's for a quarter.

Nevertheless, in accordance with P.B.'s instructions, my father liquidated his assets in this country and determined to move to Montevideo, Uruguay, to avoid the nuclear fallout from the Third World War just in case P.B.'s efforts with his Sirian companions proved no match for the forces of darkness. (P.B. seems, for the moment, to have been successful.) In a letter to me written in September 1959, P.B. stated, in typically oblique fashion: "My own work in connection with the international situation comes to an end so far as outward activity is concerned, at the end of this month." This of course led us to expect even greater "inward" activity devoted to procuring peace for our planet.

P.B. did not decide there was going to be a Third World War on the basis of the world situation or by any reasoned method. His was not an *opinion;* it was a revelation. P.B. had been *told* there was going to be a war by the very higher powers that were doing their best, presumably with P.B. as their human instrument, to stop it.

What, precisely, was involved in any given revelation was never made clear. Nor did anybody feel courageous enough to ask P.B. the obvious questions: Who revealed it to you? When? How, exactly, did it happen? Can you talk directly to these forces? Have you any control over the discussions? *Are* they discussions? Give me an exact description of the unfolding of a revelation, from the time it begins until the time it ends. Any request for concrete information threatened the fantasy world in which P.B. lived and that he demanded that others inhabit as well, at least if those others were to be his disciples.

Many people at that time believed a war was imminent—some built air raid shelters—but few thought they could prevent it by meditation. What, then, did P.B. do to make himself think he was communing with powers from another planet (or another "plane," as he often put it) to stop a war? He did not pretend he was involved in any cosmic conference, though it would have been in consonance with his behavior. It is not as if he would walk into a board room with a name tag saying P.B., PLANET: EARTH, put down his black nonleather briefcase, and say, "Now, gentlemen, where were we?" He must have truly felt that during meditation he was "in touch" with some higher force and that his contact with that force was beneficial to the world.

As usual, P.B. insisted on mystery, and secrecy, and hints, and mysterious smiles. And again the question must be put: Was he kidding my uncle Bernard, and my father Jacques, and his other disciples as well as himself, or just them? Did he consciously know that he was engaged in play-acting, or did he convince himself that he was doing what he claimed to be doing? If he really believed he was communing with some higher power, why all the mumbo-jumbo?

Of course, one had to excuse P.B. not telling the rest of the world. They would simply have ridiculed him. He could hardly take out an ad in the *New York Times* and expect to be taken seriously. Certainly, he implied, he wished he could warn the whole of humanity of the danger it was facing, but the whole of humanity would only laugh at him. The whole of humanity was intent on destroying itself. He could only work behind the scenes to avert disaster and at the same time fulfill his obligation to his closest disciples by warning them of the danger he foresaw, urging them to liquidate all their business in North America and Europe and make a permanent move to South America.

We were all forbidden to discuss the situation with "ordinary" people. In effect, my parents were asked to believe that a catastrophic war was imminent and at the same time that they must not, under any circumstances, alert their own families to the impending disaster. This was a lot to ask, and I think it led to permanent bitter feelings. I knew that P.B. and his disciples believed that the world as we knew it was about to end. I never thought this through, however.

I can remember at various times wanting to "save" friends, wanting to talk to some of them about "the war." But I thought they would never believe me. This was undoubtedly true. Still, I remember feeling both horrified and sad that the war would engulf everybody but those of us who were preparing for it.

P.B., meanwhile, was proving more and more elusive. He was not eager to correspond with his disciples. In fact, he wrote to his son on January 26, 1960, to say that he was no longer able to get involved in questers' and readers' personal lives, affairs, or spiritual problems. He was not to be diverted from time-and-energy-requiring aims that would affect the fate of millions of others. He told his son to hold out no hope that he would write to anyone or even that he could get in touch with him soon. This was an emergency.

For many of P.B.'s disciples, the move to South America presented a formidable task. Many were poor. Typical were the Ted and Sara Barner family and their children, Robert and Edward. They were organic farmers, dedicated to P.B., and loyal to him. They barely eked out a living on their small farm in Fallbrook, California, where they grew a variety of organic vegetables. They were poor and unsophisticated. Ted had a lip cancer that was getting worse every year, which he refused to treat by medical means. He attempted every possible quack cure, especially fasting. For them to move to South America, leaving the rest of their nonspiritual family behind, was a major and potentially devastating prospect, but they felt they had no choice. They believed in P.B. absolutely, without reservation. Had not P.B. looked at Sara with such intensity that she knew he could read her thoughts? They left before my parents did. They decided to move to a small valley outside of Quito, Ecuador, where they had heard there was an ideal climate and fine farming. Even though they were eventually disappointed in P.B. and went through difficult times, they never lost their devotion to him.

It is much to my uncle Bernard's credit that, unlike any other disciple, he was not afraid to criticize P.B. He did so often. By 1956, these criticisms were beginning to take a more angry tone. On August 11, 1956, he wrote to P.B.:

My esteem for you has sunk to its very lowest point. It is plain that you are an Egoist of the first water. It is also quite catching! When I brought my brother Jack to you ten years ago, he had a profound desire to be of some use to humanity. Look at him now, he writes me letters only of his deals in business, of his and his family's doings. His philanthropic ideas are buried under ten years of your teachings. He intends to enjoy himself to the very last and then when you divulge the location which will be safe for survival, he will emigrate there in style and build a fine house and invite you as his guest, where you will stay permanently; slowly Diana will compel you to comply with her household routine and you will have heartburn and liver attacks from eating her psychically-charged indigestible food, while you tell them amusing stories at dinner time. I should call that a fit epitome to your life and teachings.

Bernard was right. My parents did in fact intend to build a home in Uruguay and invite P.B. to live with us. They offered this to him in a letter dated August 23, 1958:

Naturally P.B. we sincerely hope that you will be able to live with us, and if it is preferable for you, we could have a separate house on the same estate for yourself. Diana and I have talked this over and if that is not satisfactory, then we would like as a second choice to buy a place for you. Please do not worry about the financial part of it, as we will take care of that.

Uncle Bernard made a similar offer, though at a slightly less exalted level, commensurate with his finances. He was critical of P.B. because he suspected P.B. would eventually divulge to my parents, but not to him, the place for survival. But Bernard still clearly believed that P.B. actually did *know* where that place was, and that it would be needed. He was absolutely convinced that P.B. was powerful, even if he misused his power. For Bernard, it was not that P.B. merited these powers—he simply, somehow, *had* them. Even at his most angry, Bernard still believed that P.B. was in contact with higher powers. Why did he find this belief impossible to shake? Would it have made his life pointless and absurd? In the same letter he recognizes how ridiculous P.B.'s little obsessions were: "tying pieces of string together for two hours, so as to yield four feet of string wherewith to tie a bundle—or sending your secretary to exchange a 10 cent article in downtown N.Y., which cost him $1.20 in carfare—or saving bits of paper, untyped pieces of envelopes, etc., on which to write your ideas, etc., etc., etc."

P.B. responded to the accusation about the string with good humor, telling Bernard that he must admit that in comparison with the terrible blows on the head that the medieval Tibetan guru Milarespa had received and that knocked him unconscious, his suffering while seated comfortably in a revolving chair for two hours tying the string was a much lighter test. However, the tone of tongue-in-cheek was not entirely genuine. P.B. did talk of tests that were constantly being set for his disciples and constantly being flunked. He admitted that he often set tests for his disciples, asking them for something "apparently" unnecessary. Then when they refused, he would give them to understand that the request was a test and they had flunked.

Bernard wrote again to say that "throughout the years I have pointed out to you time and again the various predictions you have made which have not materialized. I have a list of about twenty such predictions." Even when Bernard was giving P.B. factual information, he could not prevent himself from complaining, as if he were trying to settle scores with a negligent or cruel or nonomnipotent and therefore disappointing father.

But in this case, Bernard felt that P.B. had information he wanted to keep secret. This enraged Bernard, both because he felt important facts were being kept back from him and because he felt it was a sadistic game. He decided to play it as well: "Now I come to what can be called the 'esoteric' side of my information. Let me whisper it to you in your ear, for it is 'hush-hush' stuff! There is a region in South America, with its topographical character of such a curious and unique nature as to make this spot virtually immune (but completely so!) from every combination of nuclear hazards, whether it be fallout radiation, or anything else. The only spot on earth to which it can be compared is Lhasa, Tibet, but without the latter's manifold disadvantages. But listen—this is going to be good! Imagine my intense surprise when studying this region in my thoughts, to find that there is a rumor that in this very area, (Refuge XL) a group of oriental or asiatic mystics (could it be Tibetans?) have already established themselves secretly. I can say no more." Later in the letter he tells P.B., "I must withhold all information on this subject until I see you personally and get your promise of silence."

It was too tantalizing for P.B. to withstand (all that talk of Tibetan masters), and he took the bait. He began immediately to besiege Bernard with requests for more information. He simply must disclose the name of the place. He could be trusted to keep a secret, and so on. On October 24, 1956, P.B. wrote to ask: "Is Refuge XL Lake Titicaca where Peru and Bolivia meet and where every occult leader in Europe tells me that Tibetan adepts had built their lamasery. If this is true, then *please say so definitely.*" Because P.B. was half convinced that Bernard had gotten hold of esoteric information, he wanted to be part of it. He told Bernard that it should be kept secret from the public and from other questers but not from him.

Bernard had told P.B. that he had devised a very elaborate plan of survival for the "ordinary" questers (presumably everybody except Bernard, Ida, and P.B.), but refused to hand over the plan to P.B. unless P.B. would come to him personally to obtain it. He tantalized P.B. with excerpts from it. I doubt it was even written down. I think it was a means of teasing P.B.

Teasing had always played an important role in our family. My father's father was a terrible tease, and so was my father. Evidently it was popular in Bukhara. A tease was most successful when the person was actually frightened. Teasing often had sadistic and sexual undertones. Bernard clearly had in mind several thousand questers, all seeking refuge somewhere in the world. In fact, less than a dozen people were involved. Bernard saw himself as a "group director" who, so he told P.B. on November 6, 1956, "will be responsible for finding the suitable location for future life of the group, with the help of the higher powers."

Although P.B. had originally narrowed down the choice to South America, he continually hinted that it might be necessary, for mysterious reasons, to change plans. He wrote my father and Bernard saying that information had come to him, and developments had occurred, that might make it necessary to tell everybody to go someplace else. He was awaiting further developments. There was mystery, always mystery, and secrecy, with implications of direction from the higher powers.

Slowly it began to dawn on the questers that there was something a little bit suspicious about these higher powers. For a guru, P.B. seemed inordinately interested in what he termed "practical affairs" but that appeared to everybody else to be harebrained schemes. In 1957, he wrote to Bernard to investigate, when in Ecuador, "a business in which I am personally interested in starting. This is the drying of bananas for export trade, as well as for storing for home use." For what possible reason could the higher powers be concerned with dried bananas?

Bernard and Ida finally did move to Brazil, to a small farming community outside São Paolo. P.B. thought it would be safest to live on a farm, so that there would always be food in the event of a worst-case scenario. From there, they attempted in vain to interest P.B. in the place. P.B. answered everybody's letters but remained aloof, seemingly unable to make up his mind where he should go. He responded from New York on December 21, 1958, that as usual he was engaged in an activity requiring great secrecy, at the very highest levels, involving the fate of our planet. P.B. was not to be budged.

Bernard wrote him a series of letters with more and more grievances from the past. He complained that P.B. had stayed with him in Cuernavaca to write a book but never wrote a line. The book he finally did write, *The Spiritual Crisis of Man*, according to Bernard, "was an inducement to sleep, no doubt because you wrote it in Jack and Di's house, where you were deprived of proper nourishment." In spite of his complaints, Bernard was still hooked in and could not let go. He told P.B. that he and Ida had left all their property to him in the case of their death. He said he did this on the very day he learned that P.B. had told everybody, except him, where to go to escape the nuclear disaster. The letters sound as though they come from a deeply hurt son.

My parents decided to move to Montevideo. Linda and I were still attending high school at our boarding school, La Villan. I was convinced that my parents were right to leave America. Since we had been taking Spanish in school, we were looking forward to living in Uruguay. The world we had known was going to end, but we would be safe. I don't think I ever really believed that the world as such would end. I thought of it more as an adventure story, a metaphorical struggle between the forces of evil and the spiritual forces of good. That real people would actually die never occurred to me. The coming war was more of an idea, a test, a theory, a vision, than an actual event. I believe now that all of us—me, Linda, and my parents—were never entirely convinced that P.B. was right.

Still, here we were, moving our lives about to accommodate his vision. We arrived in Montevideo in 1959. I was eighteen, my sister fifteen. My parents were waiting for us in an airy, sunny, apartment they had just bought.

My parents wanted to find a *chacra*, a farm, about an hour away from Montevideo. Since I spoke Spanish and quickly began making Uruguayan friends, I was asked to find the farm. I must have visited about fifty farms, looking for the perfect refuge. Finally I found one with five thousand mature fruit trees on 150 acres of fertile ground on the banks of a large river. I negotiated the sale, and we had our farm. But my parents could not bring themselves to move. We had a lovely apartment across the street from the golf club in Montevideo, and life there was both cheap and good. We kept the farm as a kind of insurance and continued to live in the city. We also bought a parcel of land in the beach resort of Punta del Este, some one hundred miles west of Montevideo, where we spent the summer and my parents decided to build a resort home.

P.B. meanwhile was seemingly not yet ready to join his disciples. He kept making exploratory trips to other parts of the world. The disciples living in South America were beginning to resent this, since they had only moved there on his recommendation. In all his letters to us he spoke about joining us any day, but in subsequent letters he would postpone the trip by just a few more weeks. It began to seem as if he would never come.

In fact, P.B. never did come to South America even on a visit. Instead, he suddenly and mysteriously moved to Australia, briefly, and then to New Zealand for a longer period. Everybody was puzzled. None of the disciples knew what had happened. Later, in his book about P.B., his son Kenneth explained:

What was my father doing in Australasia? He resided in Perth, Sydney and Auckland for a combined period of three years. I feel it is now permissible to disclose the reason. He explained to me at the time that there were a handful of spiritually advanced people around the world whose mission it was to concentrate mentally during meditation upon the leaders of the chief nations. Their mission was to "pray for peace," to concentrate on raising the consciousness of the world's leaders to a level where their own higher selves could work on them for peace and restrain them from any rash warlike actions. He explained that this work was most effective if carried out in reasonable proximity to the geographical location of those leaders. I gathered that he had been allocated the task of mentally working upon Mao Zedong, the Chinese leader.

Did P.B. really believe that somebody had "allocated" such work to him? Was this a "message" he received in meditation? Did he simply take it upon himself? Is this a retrospective rationale for moving to New Zealand? One would think these "higher powers" would have had more direct and effective methods of communicating with the Chinese leader.

P.B.'s disciples felt abandoned, some even tricked. Especially my uncle and the family in Ecuador. They had not only turned their lives upside-down for him, they had destroyed themselves financially to follow his instructions and move to South America. And now the guru was not coming. Their disappointment and, in the case of Bernard, anger were palpable. It seemed like a cruel joke. What if P.B. had new and more vital information that he had decided not to share with anybody, even his oldest disciples? To the disciples, it had the feel of a gang leader who tells the rest of his gang where to meet in order to split up the gold, then runs off in a different direction with the gold, never to be seen again. In this case, the gold was the information on the war. Everybody was convinced the war was imminent and that P.B. had privileged access to vital information. He would know before anybody else when D-day was. But now suddenly he was not sharing this crucial information. For the disciples, it was a deep abandonment, a permanent and transformative disappointment. Nothing would ever be quite the same again. It never seemed to occur to them that the real disappointment was that there was no "information" to share. Maybe P.B. felt he had gotten in over his head, with all these people changing their lives to follow his words.

P.B.'s disappearance was much less of a blow to my parents than it was to the other disciples. For one thing, they were wealthier, and although my father had liquidated his business in America, he had enough cash to make new investments. My family was not immensely rich, but we were certainly not poor. Life in Montevideo was fairly sophisticated. My parents made friends rather easily, especially my mother, and Linda and I were happy in a new and Spanish-speaking country. My parents took up golf, I started attending the Universidad de Montevideo, and Linda finished high school. We all seemed less and less worried about the world ending. I think each of us was beginning to believe in P.B.'s vision less and less.

Before Linda and I had left Switzerland, my parents decided to make a tour of the major South American countries that were considered suitable for migration: Chile, Peru, Ecuador, Uruguay, and Argentina. They had been considering settling in Chile because the climate and food most resembled California's. The ship my parents took from Italy to South America stopped first in Uruguay; my parents took a tour of the capital city of Montevideo and found a suburb, Carrasco,

that reminded them of Southern California. Uruguay was known as
the Switzerland of South America. They were favorably impressed.
The next day the ship docked in Buenos Aires, a few hours away
from Montevideo.

In Buenos Aires, the capital of Argentina, walking along the
fashionable main shopping street, Calle Florida, my parents saw an
interesting and elegant-looking store, Joyeria Guthman. They
walked in and were wandering about, when a very tall man with an
extraordinarily large nose approached and asked in heavily accented
Spanish if he could help. It was clear he was French, and so my father
answered him in French. Within minutes he asked them to come into
the back room. He was Freddi Guthman; this was his jewelry shop. "I
hate it," he told them. "But what can I do; it is my Jewish heritage."

"I know what you mean," said my father. "I am Jewish, and I too
am in jewelry. The thing I like about it, though, is that I get to go to
India often. Have you ever been?"

"India?" said Freddi. "You go to India?"

"Oh yes. In fact, my son Jeffrey and I were in India last year."

"Where were you?" he asked, slowly.

"Oh, lots of places—Madras, Calcutta, Bombay, Trivandrum."

There was a stunned silence. Freddi called in a French-Russian
Jewish woman whom he introduced as his wife Natascha. "Natascha,
listen. I think something important is about to happen. Tell Natascha
where you were again in India."

We repeated the list. They looked at each other. "Trivandrum?"
said Natascha. "What were you doing there?"

"We went to visit an Indian sage by the name of Krishnamenon
or Gurunathan."

Freddi jumped up, came over to my parents, stooped from his
almost seven-foot height, put his arms around my small father, and
wept. "Come," he said, "I am closing the store. We have to go to our
house. There is much we must talk about."

It turned out that Freddi and Natascha were the leading figures
in a group of about twenty Argentine disciples of Krishnamenon, all
of whom had spent considerable time in India in Trivandrum. This
day began a long and intense friendship between my parents and

many of these disciples, especially with Freddi and Natascha, who to this day remain my parents' closest friends.

Freddi had also been on a quest in India. He had read P.B.'s books and visited the Maharshi. Then he had gone to Almora, in the Himalayas, meditating and talking with the Ramakrishna monks there. When he met Krishnamenon, he knew he had found his guru. Freddi was a talented writer, a poet, and an extraordinary conversationalist. He and Natascha were to become like a second family to us.

Montevideo is just across the river from Buenos Aires, where Krishnamenon's disciples lived. My parents spent one week with "the disciples," as we came to call them, staying up all night and talking about matters spiritual. When Linda and I arrived in Montevideo in March 1959, one of the first things we did was take a trip to Buenos Aires to meet my parents' friends. We loved one another on sight and began to visit frequently. The discussion was always about India, spirituality, mysticism, P.B., and Gurunathan. The disciples ridiculed the idea of a world war. They also began to ask us probing questions about P.B. My parents recognized that much of what they had been taught sounded absurd when repeated to a group of skeptical but sympathetic intellectuals who were nonetheless committed to spiritual values.

A close disciple of Krishnamenon, John Levy, came to Buenos Aires in 1959, and everybody was much taken with him, especially me and my mother. (She was eventually to become his "disciple," but *My Mother's Guru* is another book.) He was an enormously wealthy, irascible, upper-class Englishman who was sometimes unbearably rude and sometimes extraordinarily sweet. I was fascinated with him and wrote P.B. in Australia an obnoxious letter on December 14, 1959:

Dear P.B.:

This letter shall affect to a very large extent my destiny and therefore I consider it of the utmost importance.

We have just returned from Buenos Aires where we went in order to attend the talks on Vedanta given by John Levy. I had several very long private conversations with him through which I have come to the opinion that he is a realized being.

The results of these talks are that I am to go to England, probably in early March of 1960 for a 2 fold reason. One is that John Levy claims to be able to give me the Truth, and of course this comes before all, and is always the first consideration in my life. The second reason is to enter a Tutorial college in or around London in order to prepare myself for the entrance examination to either London University or Oxford and for the General Certification of Education Examination. John Levy feels that in my case a first-class education is as necessary as my spiritual development. Mom and Dad are at a loss as to what they should do. They also feel that a good worldly education is absolutely necessary, which I cannot get here, and yet they fear the coming war and don't want us to be separated. I feel that in case of war I would manage to get back in time. Besides I cannot go on neglecting both my spiritual and normal education for the fear of a possible war.

This is an urgent and very important matter, and it is to you, P.B., that we turn for advice. Your answer shall have much to do with our decision.

Please, please, write us with the least possible delay, for my future may depend on your letter.

With faith and devotion,
Jeff

I don't know what P.B. responded. Clearly I was almost ready to abandon his idea that a Third World War was imminent. But I wasn't quite brave enough to do so just yet.

The Buenos Aires disciples considered that P.B. was on a rather low level, philosophically speaking, and tried to convince my father that he should return to India to see Krishnamenon. My father agreed, and poor P.B. received yet another letter from the apostasy-prone Masson family, this one from my father on January 15, 1959:

Dear P.B.

I have a very important question to ask you and would very much appreciate an answer so my mind can be at peace. Would you consider it disloyal if I went to Trivandrum to hear Krishnamenon's talks? As you must know I have always been very devoted and loyal to you and shall always continue to be so. Still this will probably be my last chance to hear him as first he is getting old, and second because of travel restrictions for the very near future. I am hungry for Truth and will be dissatisfied until I become Aware. What is the stumbling block? I would have to take Diana and Jeff with me, as Di insists on going and Jeff told me if I went to India without him, he would resort to any measures and meet me there, so he's really serious. Poor little Linda, though she would like a trip to India, this one would be no fun—to sit in Trivandrum and listen to lectures on Advaita—so this is a big problem.

Contrary to everybody's expectations, P.B. was not crushed and seemingly had little problem with my father's defection. He responded with a reasonable and friendly telegram saying that my father was completely free to attend the lectures and even to become a disciple of Krishnamenon. P.B. did not mention that the question of World War III was beginning to be quietly dropped. Nobody appeared to believe in it very strongly any longer—including, it would seem, P.B. himself.

My father was also, like Bernard, building up a certain resentment against P.B., as is clear from a letter he wrote to him while visiting Lima, Peru, on February 22, 1959:

Dear P.B.

Your letter of January 30th, 1959 sent to Peru was forwarded to me in Chile and waiting there upon our arrival. I will now try to answer your letter of January 30th.

1. Although it is true that a number of years ago you wrote and told everyone to feel free of any obligation towards you, you never told me that personally, and I always took it for granted that you were my guru, as you had officially accepted me as such in December of 1945 in Mysore. Although I visited India a number of times I don't think I was consciously seeking for another teacher.

2. I am very glad to see that you endorse Krishna Menon's teaching. I am writing him for permission to attend his lectures. The four of us intend to go there. Since it's impossible to make the March 15th sessions, I was told by the disciples that the next session will be sometime either in July or September. I know it is a bad month to visit India, but we can't help it. Shall let you know further when I hear from him.

3. The question of disloyalty came up because I did think you were my guru and this has been clarified by your letter and telegram about which I will talk later.

4. I will keep in mind the limitations of Krishna Menon's teaching and try to balance it with the philosophical path that I have learned from you.

5. I was quite surprised to read in your letter "I'm not even making plans about South America. If however I do so, it will be on the new basis mentioned in earlier letters." Do you mean to say that it is possible you may not come here at all? In which case, does this mean you may choose another country or remain in the U.S.A., or do you mean that you have great hopes for the "Peace Work" and that it will be safe to stay in America?

I think this is as far as my father could go toward criticizing P.B., who clearly still functioned, at least in his mind and heart, as his guru. My father was clearly aghast at what he regarded as P.B.'s abandonment of all his devoted pupils. He had for years now encouraged all of them to move to South America. It was implicit that he would join them in one or another of the countries, perhaps even float among all of them, visiting. In the event, he let everybody depart, and then he went his own way, disregarding his earlier advice and more or less refusing to explain his choice to anyone. Nobody entirely understood it, but everybody felt let down. Maybe P.B. had had enough of being a guru.

I myself wrote P.B. a typically pretentious letter on August 20, 1959, from Montevideo, Uruguay, in which I told P.B. that upon meeting the disciples in Buenos Aires, I saw that "they had attained to a very high level." The books they advocated, mostly the two quoted earlier by Krishnamenon, made a profound impression on me. I blamed P.B. for keeping me at a lower level, the "yogic standpoint," instead of on this loftier plane of Vedantic theory, and for having kept me and my family from what I felt was our right: access to a different kind of philosophical teaching. I was echoing my father: Why didn't you teach us this level? Did you even know it? It was definitely my first move against this guru, though not yet against the idea of a guru. I was merely exchanging one for another. I also implicitly criticized P.B. for encouraging us to emigrate to avoid the war. He took all of this rather good-naturedly and wrote me later in 1959:

This brings up a point which you might not have appreciated before your Vedantic studies, whether all this fuss about survival is justified. On the New Year card which the family sent me, and I was glad to have, you or Diana had written: We came to South America to preserve the body—only to find after all: we have no body, we are no body. This is pure Vedantic truth, of course, but it is also a good joke!

I was, albeit glacially, beginning to mature. I was becoming increasingly skeptical of the idea of an imminent Third World War. At the Universidad de Montevideo, I had a large number of English and Uruguayan friends; my sexuality was beginning to awaken; at long last I felt the urge to leave my family. I finally decided to apply to college. I chose Harvard and determined to leave Uruguay. Nobody put any pressure on me to stay. World War III was becoming an embarrassment, a symbol of our former selves. Clearly nobody in our family believed in it any longer. I brought it up; we all indicated that it was no longer something on which to base our lives. My parents had commitments in South America, but it was clear that they, and Linda too, intended to leave sometime during the coming year.

My father decided to give me a last trip together, to Europe, in the summer of 1961, just before I left for Harvard. We went to Germany, he bought me a Volkswagen bug, and we headed to the tip of Italy to take a ferry to Greece. My illusions were falling fast. I was beginning to give up on P.B. Even though he insisted in his letters that the war could still come, it was clear he had made a major miscalculation and had caused all of us major disruptions in our lives. But I was still convinced that even if P.B. was not the right guru for me, gurus as such, and "philosophy"—that is, Indian philosophy—were my life. I wanted to study Sanskrit. In Uruguay I had had a number of girl-friends, and although I had not slept with anybody yet, I could feel I was getting closer. This was in such contrast to the teaching of P.B. that I had to decide either that he was wrong or that I was immoral and sinful. Sex seemed to be such a powerful force, I could not dream of controlling it. It was time to start a new life.

I was still young for my age—physically, intellectually, socially, and even morally. This is evident from an entry in my diary for New Years Day, 1960:

New Years Resolutions:
Memorize *Atma Nirvritti* and *Atma Darshan*
Improve table manners

In August 1961, I left for Cambridge and my first year as an under-graduate at Harvard.

Chapter Nine

Harvard and Disillusion

In late August 1961, at nineteen, I arrived in Cambridge to study English literature, especially modern poetry. I was put in a freshman dormitory but felt completely out of place. I could not imagine surviving a year in such an environment. Part of the reason is that I was so young for my age. I had almost no social skills and really couldn't talk to boys my own age. I felt completely lost in the very first discussions I heard. I could not participate and knew I would never be accepted.

So I went to see the chairman of the department of English, Walter Jackson Bate. With unbelievable chutzpah, I told him that I had already studied English literature at the University of Montevideo and that I should be given a year's credit for the reading I had done. I cannot imagine why, but after an hour's conversation, Professor Bate told me he accepted my work and that I would be given one year's credit. I could henceforth be considered a second-year student at Harvard.

A few hours later I was on my way to Adams house, where I was put in a small suite with two other students, Bob and Louis. Even there I felt different, unacceptable. I was a vegetarian and there was not much for me to eat. I remember meeting Sol Kripke, the philosopher, who was kosher, and we managed to find some solace eating together a few times. But I felt completely out of place in the college environment. It was quickly apparent to me that I was far less mature both intellectually and socially than almost anybody else I met. My way of compensating for this was to deny it totally and claim that things were the opposite of what they seemed: I couldn't get on with kids my own age because I was so intellectually and socially mature. I really needed to be with adults.

I was also having trouble with the so-called parietal rules at Harvard which said that a woman must leave a student's room by 10 P.M. Every second that I was not studying, I spent at Wellesley, meeting women. This was a paradox that was becoming more and more pronounced in my character: While I still considered myself a spiritual person, I was becoming increasingly obsessed—an even stronger word would not be out of place—with sex. I saw it everywhere. I wanted it. I thought about it all the time. No woman seemed safe from my predations. I look back at it with horror. I had absolutely no understanding of what I was doing.

One evening I was invited to meet an older (perhaps forty-five) professor of Indian philosophy who was visiting from India. She had something of a following in India and was even considered a kind of guru. Somehow the discussion turned to spiritual matters. This woman said she had never felt sexual desire in her life because her mind was filled with spiritual thoughts. There was simply no room. As the guests were leaving her apartment, she asked me to stay a little bit, as there was something she wanted to tell me. When we were alone she said: "You looked as though you did not believe what I was saying. Is that true?"

"Well, actually I don't, no," I replied.

"You don't believe I am free of sexual desire?"

"No."

"I will prove it to you. Touch my breasts."

I did as I was told.

"See, I feel nothing. Now touch my thighs."

I did as I was told.

"Again, nothing. Even if you enter me with your penis, I will feel nothing. Do you believe me?"

"No."

"Try."

I did.

"See, I feel nothing sexual. The whole time this is going on I am thinking only about the higher self, the atman."

I was skeptical. I assumed it was a ruse to have sex. I wondered if this was what P.B. told his wife, if gurus generally did this. It did not occur to me then that I was not conducting research but was engaged in a human encounter for which I had responsibilities, too.

By this time I was taking courses in Sanskrit, which proved extraordinarily difficult. I knew Spanish and French but had never before learned an inflected language, and Sanskrit is highly inflected. The little bit of Sanskrit I had learned as a young boy did not help here. I didn't know anything about cases, and when I was told a noun form I did not recognize was a dative or an ablative or a genitive, I had no idea what was meant. Another blow to my narcissism. It took me years to understand that verbs are conjugated and nouns are declined. To this day, I mix it up and am never sure where declensions and conjugations belong. The man who taught the class was a very patrician Virginian, Daniel H. H. Ingalls, Wales Professor of Sanskrit at Harvard.

I remember meeting Professor Ingalls for the first time:

"Hi," I said. "I'm Jeff. Who are you?"

"Professor Ingalls."

"What do I call you?"

"Professor Ingalls."

I was in his office, and he said he had to leave.

"Where are you going?"

Puzzled by my inquisitiveness, which I don't believe he had encountered before, he replied that he was going to get a haircut.

"I can come with you," was my eager response.

He was bemused.

"We could go for a drive afterward to see the fall leaves change colors."

He had no idea where I had come from. And I had no idea what Harvard was like.

"Before you leave, who is your guru?"

He was completely mystified. "If you mean who taught me Sanskrit, it was Professor Clark."

"No, I mean your spiritual teacher."

"I don't have one" was his dry response. It was really the first inkling I had that somebody could teach and study Sanskrit for reasons other than spiritual. It was a completely new notion for me.

Sanskrit as a language, rather than a collection of spiritually freighted terms, was also a new concept to me. If it had not been for the kindness of one of the students, Alan Keiler, then a junior fellow in linguistics and now a professor of musicology at Brandeis, I doubt I would have made it past the first year. He was very talented in languages and was amused by my complete mystification. He set about coaching me and teaching me the rudiments of the language so that I could follow what was going on in class. He succeeded, barely. I also turned for help to Wendy Donniger, now professor of religious studies at the University of Chicago.

After less than a year at Adams house, I decided I needed to live off campus. There were rules about women not spending the night that I found hard to obey. It was only a matter of time, I thought, before I got caught. I could not believe that the university would really care, but friends told me it was serious and I had better be careful. I talked the Center for the Study of World Religions into letting me stay there in a lovely subsidized garden apartment. As an undergraduate, I had no business being there, but somehow I convinced them. It seemed a shortcut to knowledge. I was so helpless there (as a child spiritual star I had not been expected to cook or clean) that Arthur, the caretaker, took pity on me, and began helping me take care of the apartment. He was one of the sweetest men I had ever met. Once there I met the person with whom I was closest in my academic life: Bimal Matilal, an Indian who, until he died a few months ago at fifty-six, had been Spalding Professor of Eastern Religions and Ethics at Oxford University, and the best Sanskrit scholar I knew.

In all fairness, it was Ingalls, cool as he was and remained to me personally, who taught me what scholarship looked like. He was cool because I was so insistent and pushy. He saw I had talent but was lacking much, including everything he considered social graces. I knew he was extremely conservative politically, where I was not. In all fairness to him, I don't think he disliked me; he just found me intolerable, which I often was. He always encouraged my growing love for scholarship, which he certainly shared.

At the same time that Ingalls was introducing me to the real world of Indian scholarship on a daily basis, my reading of the great French indologist Louis Renou and the Belgian Buddhist scholar Étienne Lamotte showed me that what I had learned about the history of Indian texts from talking with P.B. was entirely bogus. The dates were wrong, the names were wrong, even the language was wrong. P.B. didn't know whether a text had been written in Sanskrit or in some other language. My judgment was improving, I was maturing intellectually, but it was also a question of exposure. You could not put P.B.'s books next to those by Renou or Lamotte and not immediately see the enormous gulf. I had never seen books like those by Renou and Lamotte in my house. I had not been exposed to anything but the world P.B. had approved. Lamotte, in contrast to P.B., knew the language; Lamotte was cautious and careful in what he said. He knew the history. He knew the texts thoroughly. P.B., as a writer about Indian texts, was simply a charlatan.

I was a charlatan too. I found that out from I. A. Richards. He was teaching a graduate course in poetry that I had absolutely no business attending. He graciously allowed me to take it. I made a complete fool of myself. It was entirely beyond my capabilities. I have just found a letter I wrote to my parents on December 6, 1962:

> In poetics, with I. A. Richards. Don't understand a word. But that's all right, because nobody else in the class does either. I spoke with him, he likes me, and wants me to do a paper on Sanskrit poetics. His course is so difficult to get into that there

is no examination. Just a paper a week. Guess what our paper is on this week? "Give a morphemic and phonemic explanation of the syntactic difference of the interpolation of 'less' for 'more' in Book I., line 388 of *Paradise Regained* by Milton." How do I do it, you ask? I bullshit.

For the essay, I wrote an embarrassingly saccharine account of the Upanishads and English poetry that made even P.B. look good by comparison. It was awful beyond description. I spoke of how Shelley had "undoubtedly" (meaning I had no idea if it was true or not) read these texts in an early translation and had "taken over their angelic substance into his own heavenly poetry." I can still remember what I. A. Richards wrote at the end of this essay, to which he gave the lowest passing grade he could (B−), out of compassion: "Of the ineffable one must speak, if at all, softly." He was referring to the fact that I was writing the equivalent of a scream. I even remember one of the lines: "Angels have brushed with their wings the Upanishads and left magic dust on them for the rest of us to enjoy." It wasn't English, it wasn't writing, it wasn't thinking, it wasn't anything. The odd thing is that the minute I. A. Richards pointed this out, I *knew* it. Something was happening. I learned too from his response to a maudlin poem I wrote him, fortunately lost. When I asked him what he thought of it some days later, he said with extraordinary finesse: "One must live with a poem for a long time before forming any kind of judgment." I knew he was sparing my feelings.

As was Ingalls when he gave me a C− in my first year of Sanskrit. He wrote on my first paper: "If I were to grade this for the promise it shows, I would give it an A or an A−. If I had to grade it by current standards, I would have to give it an F. As you see, I have compromised."

The professor of Buddhism at Harvard, Masatoshi Nagatomi, was personally much warmer and kinder to me than Ingalls. I spent many evenings at his house, ate with him, and enjoyed the hospitality of his family for many years. In spite of his personal liking for me, the message was the same. I studied Pali and Tibetan with him.

He supervised my honors thesis, a translation of a Tibetan text, lost in Sanskrit, into English. I heavily and pretentiously annotated it and poorly translated it as well. I simply didn't know enough Tibetan. Nagatomi made this painfully clear. I had attempted something far beyond my modest linguistic means. I wanted to translate it because it had never before been translated. I had visions of it going into print immediately. Nagatomi saw it going into a trash basket instead, only he was too kind to say so. It was slow and hard work, but I was beginning to become aware of my own limitations. Nevertheless, with enormous bad grace I blamed him for not seeing to it that I got a summa cum laude when I graduated from Harvard, instead of the magna cum laude which I did receive (and which was considerably more than I deserved).

I had been ill-prepared for the rigors of Harvard. I was not equipped for it intellectually. I had, in fact, meager talents for philological research. What I had in abundance was enthusiasm and soon a love of the Sanskrit language. As I began to master it, I found pleasure in actually reading and understanding a difficult text, in really *knowing* what it said, as opposed to guessing. I was never good at grammar, but I was a voracious reader, and I began to read both primary and secondary literature in Sanskrit with enormous gusto. I was slowly acquiring some knowledge. I was beginning to know something. And I was beginning to recognize when somebody else did not.

Once I spent a few hours with Alan Watts, who was visiting the Center. He looked at my bookshelves and said he was surprised at how many different kinds of books I had. Later that evening he gave a lecture about Buddhism. At one point, he used a beautiful and striking metaphor that he claimed was from the Chinese Buddhist canon. I was sitting with Masatoshi Nagatomi, who told me that this metaphor was definitely not to be found in the canon. I asked Alan Watts about it after the lecture. "Where did you get it from?" It was clear he read no Chinese. "I invented it," he said without shame.

How did I manage to go through Harvard in the sixties without ever taking a single drug? I think I was so lost in my own world that this phenomenon passed me by. But I was also very impressed with a meeting I had in 1963. I quote from a letter I wrote to my sister:

> Yesterday, Friday night, I was at Radcliffe, talking with two girls there about L.S.D., when a troubled-looking graduate girl comes over and explained that she was in the program with one T. Leary, and quit, because *it is definitely harmful to the mind and the body*. She said I had only to meet Leary myself if I wanted proof of this, for he was an example of what happens to people who take the drug. She has promised to send me the articles where this is definitely proven. I don't know whether this is so or not, but she claims that many of her friends have suffered, and I don't want to take chances. Not yet anyway, until this whole thing is more thoroughly looked into.

There was something about this woman, whom I never saw again, that convinced me that she knew something I didn't, that she had "been there," and I determined not to experiment with such a dangerous drug. Also, of course, there was the sense of superiority: What was the purpose of LSD but an attempt to bring you to a higher consciousness, which my whole life was already designed to do? To ask for such a shortcut seemed to me cowardly, and philosophically suspect. There was also something slightly sinister about the atmosphere surrounding LSD that put me off.

I see from a letter I wrote Linda a few days later that I met Leary. I had asked him to give a lecture to the Harvard Oriental Society, which was just an idea of mine so that I could call myself its president. He spoke on "Indian Mysticism and the Mescaline Experience." I told her:

> He's entirely gone, entirely mystically committed. Is even thinking of quitting Harvard, because of the "crazy game it is." Strangely enough, though, he is a striking person. Somewhat sage-like. I'm beginning to think that somewhere there must be a secret manual, entitled, "How to act like a sage and be believed," that all these people read, for otherwise, how do they manage to

imitate each other so perfectly? And in such detail? Going to the meeting at 8:30, will finish this letter when I return. It's now 2:30—just got back. It is without a doubt the most interesting evening yet spent at Harvard. Truly a remarkable intellectual experience. It was a very exciting experience. Everyone there took an active and interested part in the discussion which reached a superb level of intellectual depth, nearly everyone there said they had found it a unique meeting. Very tired now. Will write it all out tomorrow.

I never did, and I have no memory at all of the most memorable evening I spent at Harvard.

Matilal and I began reading Sanskrit texts with T.R.V. Murti, the Buddhist scholar from the Benares Hindu University. When he found out I was dating a girl, he told me he could not teach me unless I stopped. It was the Hindu tradition. I was surprised when Matilal defended him, because I always presumed he was as secular as I was rapidly becoming. But it was his tradition, and he knew it intimately. There was nothing, he explained, peculiar about Murti's comment, given that he thought of the two of us as more than ordinary students. For Murti, it was as if we were his chelas, his disciples, and he saw it as his duty to teach us more than Sanskrit. But I did not stop.

Matilal and I also read some texts with the great Sanskrit scholar V. Raghavan from Madras. He was a man much taken with himself and his knowledge of Sanskrit, which was indeed phenomenal. Matilal and I invited him to an Indian curry in my apartment, and when he arrived we were playing *The Magic Flute*. He entered, sniffed the air suspiciously (neither Matilal nor I were sterling cooks), and told us to take off the noise.

"But Professor Raghavan," I protested, "that is not noise. That is *The Magic Flute*."

"I don't care what kind of flute it is, take it off."

I later put on some Indian music, but that was not to his liking, either, since it was North Indian, and he only liked South Indian music. Before he left, I asked him what Sanskritist I might consider working with when I went to India, and he told me, "There is only one Sanskritist in India, and you are talking to him." While a great scholar, he was also a devout Hindu, and he told us proudly: "Every morning when I awake, I recite a chapter from *The Ramayana* in Sanskrit. No breakfast without *Ramayana.*" In his own way, he was as fanatical as P.B.

Edward Conze, the Buddhist scholar from England, was at Harvard at that time as well. Nagatomi and I took him out to dinner one night, during which he proceeded to destroy the reputation of his colleagues. Over dessert he hissed at his wife, who had mildly corrected him: "What do you know about such matters? You were a cleaning lady when I met you." This completely flabbergasted me and the other guests. Alan Watts, too, had been unbearably rude to his wife, bragging openly about his attraction to other women. I was beginning to wonder about these scholars of Hinduism and Buddhism. The gentleness and compassion for all beings that they read about in their texts did not seem to translate into their lives.

The more I learned about India, the more I realized how little P.B. actually knew. This began to enrage me. I felt I had been taken in, duped. It was all a trick. P.B. knew no Sanskrit, knew no texts, invented things, lied, cheated, and stole, intellectually speaking. How could I have been so stupid? In spirit, P.B. might have been like the Indian sages he idolized. His ideas may have been similar to theirs. But he did not really represent any tradition, any body of knowledge, any other person—in fact, anything at all. He was just a hodgepodge of misread and misunderstood ideas from an ancient culture he did not know or understand. In this sense he was a phony, a charlatan, a mountebank, an impostor, a quack. I couldn't find enough words to describe my disappointment.

I ranted and railed to my parents. They were fair to me, but they also defended P.B. They were interested not in scholarship but in experience. I felt it incumbent on me to *prove* to them that P.B. was a fraud. The opportunity came while I was still at Harvard, spending a summer with my parents in Cannes. P.B. was there.

I had long wondered how P.B. had become Dr. Brunton. Something about this was wrong. I knew enough now about universities to realize that P.B. could not possibly have been awarded a Ph.D. for any of his books. The fact that nowhere in his writings did he ever mention having studied at a university made me suspicious. Was it merely a marketing device, to make his books more acceptable? *Could somebody simply award himself a degree? Wasn't this illegal?* One day I decided to ask, in front of my parents. It was an awkward conversation, undoubtedly because when I finally was able to ask, at twenty-two, it was only because I really already knew, or suspected I knew, the answer. I had long thought there was no real doctorate, that the "doctor" in Dr. Brunton was a sham. But I wanted to ask him and force him to respond in front of others. I was beginning to take revenge for the kind of deception P.B. had practiced upon me.

"P.B.," I asked innocently, "what degree do you have?"

"I have a weighty academic honor."

"What is that?"

"A Ph.D."

"Where is it from?"

Long pause. Finally: "Roosevelt University in Chicago."

"When did you attend graduate school there?"

"I didn't."

"Did you have an oral examination?"

"I did not. I was awarded the degree partly on a philosophical thesis submitted that was judged as showing a capacity for original research and as making a contribution toward existing knowledge and partly in recognition of distinguished service to the cause of Oriental research."

It sounded very formal. Had he rehearsed this for just such an occasion as now? "You mean, the faculty of Oriental research awarded you this degree?"

"No, I became a candidate specifically for a doctorate of philosophy because this would be a recognition of attainment in the field that most concerned my future publications."

"Were you actually there? I mean, how did you get your degree?"

"It was mailed to me."

"Did you write a thesis?"

"Yes."

"What was it called?"

"I no longer remember."

"About India?"

"Yes."

"Involving Sanskrit?"

"Yes." But the *yes* was becoming fainter and fainter. My parents were silent, looking away in embarrassment for both of us. My cruelty was beginning to pall on me.

"Did you ever use your degree?"

"No, because there is no academic or professional post that I would accept were it to be offered me."

"Was one ever offered?"

A thin smile, silence. To my parents this signified "many." To me, it meant "no." "In any event, if I were to discard the college degree I hold, my place in world literature is assured."

World literature? The man was hallucinating. But I could not continue, much as I wished to. My parents were not amused by my supercilious manner, and I realized that what I was doing was intolerable to them. I couldn't help but ask him a final question, though: "When did you get your degree?" It was the ultimate in bad manners, and before he could answer or, more likely, remain silent, my parents brought the conversation to a close; "Jeff, this conversation is rude and unnecessary. Enough." I was triumphant; my parents, appalled.

"So what?" my father said later. "So if he doesn't have a Harvard degree? Does it make any difference?" It made a difference to me because I could remember the years of servility, the many introductions my father had made where the *doctor* was emphasized, no doubt reflecting the Jewish admiration for learning. "Here was a man who knows something," it said, a scholar, a man of the book. But P.B. was no such thing. The degree was fraudulent, the scholarship nonexistent, the learning of Sanskrit a wishful or wistful thought. P.B. knew a series, a limited series, of words in Sanskrit, not a language. He could not read the alphabet, any Indian alphabet, nor a single sentence in Sanskrit. Indeed, he would not even know if a sentence were Sanskrit or Hindi. He was completely ignorant of the language. More deeply, he was totally ignorant of the larger issues of Indian history and culture. He knew nothing of the reality of India. He inhabited a phantom India that existed only in his imagination and that of his disciples. Even as a fantasy it was impoverished, for nothing real that happened to Indians, all the despair and misery, the abuse, the disillusion, some of which was documented in texts he could not read and some of which he must himself have witnessed, would ever find a home, even a transient one, in his thinking.

I recently called Roosevelt University and spoke to the chair of the department of philosophy, as well as to the office of the president. Perhaps, I thought to myself, I have been doing P.B. an injustice. After all, many people have degrees who have done little or no scholarship. Maybe P.B. had admirers in the university who appreciated the fact, which I could not deny, that he brought Indian philosophy to the attention of Western Europe and the United States. It was sad. Nobody had heard of him. There was nothing about a Paul Brunton in any file.

By August 1945, P.B. had had note paper made up that said: "Dr. Paul Brunton." The recognition of the world may be nothing but maya, but he craved it anyway. He seemed to need it as badly as I needed to reach through my illusion to disillusion.

That final disillusion came the summer of 1967, in Cascais, Portugal. My parents were spending their summer vacation there, and P.B. joined them. It is to my parents' credit, I think, that they maintained friendly and cordial relations with P.B. The same could not be said for me. I was twenty-six at the time, at the height of my resentment for what I then perceived as the lies of my childhood with P.B. I was in my final year as a graduate student in Sanskrit at Harvard and by now knew enough Sanskrit to know that P.B. did not know any. One evening after dinner, the conversation turned to the subject of mediums. I was entirely skeptical. P.B. was not only a complete believer but gave us to understand that he knew certain things about trance mediumship that made it dangerous to engage in.

"Like what?" I said.

"The spirits that come, when called, are often half-animal, half-human, and they are antagonistic to humans because of the way they were treated while alive."

The comment was preposterous to me, and I said so.

"P.B., that's nonsense, and you know it."

P.B. was adamant: "It is true. We may submit ourselves to invading spirits of an evil order who thrust themselves upon our brains."

"P.B., excuse me for being impolite, but that is pure bullshit. You are talking plain rubbish. None of this exists, and you know it." But I wasn't really sure. Maybe he really did believe it after all.

P.B. was not the least bit angry. "No, Jeff, you are wrong." He then asked me what it would take for me to abandon my growing disbelief in the whole system that was his life. "For example, were I to cause this table to rise up in the air and float there, would that convince you?"

I suppose this was to have had even more effect since he had just talked about the dangers involved. Maybe he was hoping everybody would recoil in horror at the thought. He had his usual calm air about him, and he said it with such self-confidence that for a moment I was hesitant to answer. The table he was referring to was an immense ancient oak dining-room table, weighing several hundred pounds at least.

We were about eight people seated around the table, including my sister, my mother and father, and several guests. The challenge was simple. I accepted. "Yes, P.B., if this table were to rise in the air, I would concede my defeat. But, P.B., it is impossible. It won't happen." I wanted to save him the humiliation that I could sense was about to come. He smiled mysteriously, and I once again wondered what he had in mind with such a direct, simple, and open challenge. At last, the moment of truth seemed to have arrived for both of us. What was he planning?

P.B. asked us to place our hands on top of the table and to close our eyes. He was going to call the spirits to assist him in raising the table. We all did as instructed. P.B. began to chant some mumbo-jumbo that he claimed was Sanskrit, but of course by now I knew better. Suddenly he said he could feel the presence of the spirits in the room. "Keep your eyes tightly shut," he ordered, which I took as a signal for me to open mine. I saw everybody doing exactly as P.B. suggested, with their hands flat on the large table. Meanwhile he placed his hands underneath the tabletop and began to push up with all the strength in his little body, which was not much, causing a slight movement of the massive table. Then he said: "They are here, and they are beginning to move the table. Can you feel it?"

"Yes," came the assent from those around the table.

I could stand it no longer: "Well, I'm not surprised it is moving, since you have your hands underneath it and are pushing it."

P.B. started and gave the appearance of emerging from a trance. He looked sad and weary. Suddenly I felt small. My parents were horrified, not at the deception he had perpetrated on them but once again at my bad manners. I had to concede their point. But bad manners was one thing, fraud another. P.B. had been caught red-handed in an attempt to convince people that spirits were present, when all that was present were his own hands. I can't imagine how he would have proceeded. No amount of effort could have lifted the table into the air. I suppose he was hoping that the movement would be sufficient to quell my skepticism. Maybe he would explain that the spirits were exhausted that day, but we had all felt their presence, had we not? Maybe he thought he could somehow persuade us to believe that it had actually risen when all it had done was move. I find it hard to imagine what was going through his mind.

This incident spelled the end for me. The unmasking was complete. P.B. hardly reacted. Maybe he was relieved it had finally come: the day of reckoning. For me, P.B. was now nothing more than a charlatan, reduced to attempting carnival tricks for what he hoped would be a gullible audience. Maybe I had unnerved him or enraged him, or perhaps he was himself just too tired that day to rise to the occasion. It was a pathetic ending. I was not without feelings of guilt at having reduced him to this. It was a little bit like seeing a spiritual Napoleon pacing his island prison and dreaming of his days of glory. He who had commanded millions could not now find a single boatman to take him away. P.B., too, had—at least in his mind—been engaged in gigantic spiritual battles, commanding unseen forces from distant stars all for the good of mankind. And here in this obscure corner of Europe he could not lift a dining-room table an inch off the ground. What an ignoble end. Did he hate me? I don't know. I never saw him again.

My parents did not lose touch with him, however, for he was their friend, whatever they thought of him as a spiritual master. He had not published another book after the one in 1951, *The Spiritual Crisis of Man*, which sold few copies and was ridiculed by reviewers. His disciples had begun to fall away after the World War III debacle.

Eventually he moved to Switzerland, where he rented a tiny apartment in Vevey, on the Lake of Geneva. Here he lived in retirement and obscurity, still taking his notes, reading his mystic books, preparing his meager meals for himself and answering his ever-diminishing mail. His books were hardly read; few people asked him to speak anymore or wished to see him. My parents continued to visit him, however, and he them, mainly in Cannes in the South of France. He seemed happy, and not the least depressed at the alterations in his literary fortunes. Astonishingly, he did not seem to mind the loss of his status as a guru. He seemed pleased, even relieved, that my parents now treated him as a friend rather than as a guru. The air of mystery surrounding him became less, his secretiveness diminished, his pretensions began to vanish. He and I did not remain friends. I think the fault was primarily mine. I never attempted to see him again. In some way the disappointment went deep.

As the connection with P.B. began to loosen, however, my father's rivalry with his brother Bernard merely intensified. Bernard seemed still locked in a battle with P.B., unable to relinquish him as a guru and keep him as a friend. Perhaps he had invested too much, or perhaps there was little else for him. My father, now living in the South of France, decided to attempt shock therapy on Bernard, with a "Wake Up Bernard" letter dated March 20, 1965:

Wake up Bernard! Wake up before it's too late. Come out of your cocoon now. You have buried yourself long enough, Bernard, and it is about time you woke up. You really should try and see Dr. Mira Schneider in Buenos Aires. She is a very good friend of ours and has been a tremendous help to me. She has released me from my inhibitions and complexes. Go and see her and unload yourself completely. She is a very great woman and may not be in this world much longer as she is very sick. So take advantage while she is still here. She is more than a psychiatrist, since she herself has found the Truth.

Now Bernard, you must face some facts. P.B. is not the great Guru you have made him out to be all these years. Actually, he ruined your life and almost ruined mine. When I first went to see him in Mysore he agreed to be my Guru, saying that he had only accepted one disciple before me. Then a year later he told me he was not a Guru. He even gave me financial advice saying that since I was in a lucky cycle, I could speculate in the stock market. This caused me about a $25,000 loss in the Cotton future in Palm Springs. Remember? Once when he saw a house he insisted upon buying it. When I pointed out to him that he should wait, he told me: "Look here, when one sees his Guru he recognizes him instantly. In the same way, I know this house is ideally suited to me." A couple of days later I put a deposit of $1,000 on the house which I lost because it turned out to be unsuitable for him after all.

P.B. told me he was definitely going to South America. I even gave him a small amount of Peruvian money to facilitate his immediate needs upon arrival there, only to learn that he went in the exact opposite direction when he did leave the United States.

Now let's analyze some of his disciples: K didn't even confide in him when he got married. W is a superstitious and pitiful fool. D is a complete failure considering the brilliant future he had as an up and coming lawyer in Chicago. E left P.B. at an early stage. G is weak and vacillating. R has shut herself up in an ashram. H, the bearded poet, is a real nut.

When I was in India to see P.B. I wanted to go and see the Maharishi. P.B. discouraged me and I missed a great experience.

When I went to Fallbrook I became a servant to P.B., paid for the rent and running the house, cooked his meals and even waited on him and his guest Miss Kirkpatric. I was delegated the smallest room in the house for which I was paying the rent. I remember I had to go sideways in order to get into my bed, the room was so small. The strain of all that caused me the worst attack of ulcers I ever had in my life. Years before you instilled in me a reverence and awe for him as a Demi-God. Nobody could have been more loyal and sincere than I was. I even gave up sex after he told me that by doing so I could awaken the Kundalini.

I had a very valuable piece of land in the heart of Los Angeles, my tenant being Standard Oil of California. I sacrificed it in blind faith and also sold my other real estate holdings in Los Angeles which would be worth ten times more today, to follow him to South America. I blame myself for being a fool. Luckily with the proceeds of the sale I bought some Tel and Tel which saved me from utter ruin. (I was going to sell my Tel & Tel when I reached South America, but fortunately I waited.)

All these things I do not remember in bitterness. I believe that P.B. himself is a sincere seeker and an exceptionally fine human being. I believe rather that all his followers, myself included, read into him the role of a genuine Guru which he is not. I am still very fond of him and know my misfortunes are due to my own gullibility and indiscrimination. For a real genuine Guru, one who really can take you and place you into the center of your Being, there is no sacrifice too great. But P.B. himself was never that Guru. Although it is naturally a disillusion to me it was a sharp awakening so that I no longer follow blindly. P.B. himself later repeated again and again that he was a seeker, but we all made him into a Mahatma. He made me expect to get an illumination any minute. He told me about a woman shaking his hand and going into sublime peace. He told me that 90% of his students had mystical experiences (for whatever that is worth). I became a piece of putty. He told me that one meditation with him is enough, yet I meditated with him many many times. Nothing.

Bernard, you must face life. Bernard, stop and think what you are doing in a small village in Brazil. You followed P.B.'s advice now for over 20 years. You must see things in their proper perspective. You are wasting yourself and your life. You know P.B. always makes contradictory statements and when he makes a big mistake he says: "I'm sorry." Sometimes he even denied the facts.

You are in a rut escaping life. Get out before it is too late. Father degenerated completely when he retired. He had nothing to absorb his interests or keep him active and slowly life ebbed out of him. You are much too young and intelligent to withdraw completely from the world.

I am writing you this letter because my heart hurts me when I think of you.

As you see, we are still in Hong Kong. We are leaving next week for Japan and Los Angeles. If you wish to answer me, you can write to me in Los Angeles and mark it personal. I will be there the whole month of April. Otherwise you can write to the Paris address and Jeff will forward it to me.

Give my love to Ida. There is a possibility that we might visit you, with Vicki and Avram, toward the end of this year.

Jack.

Bernard wrote back a spirited defense of P.B. and sent copies of both letters to P.B. On May 31, 1966, P.B. responded to Bernard by saying that he thought my father had some justification for resentment over the unfulfilled predictions and the unsound financial advice. He hoped Jacques had received something spiritual to compensate, but evidently he had not. He acknowledged that he had made mistakes and would try to compensate Jacques in the only way he knew, and that was to remember him prayerfully during the daily period of coming out from meditation, when the divine presence is very strongly felt. There may be little or no result from it in this incarnation, but in the long term P.B. thought it would not be wasted effort.

This was a remarkably mild response to having his entire life called into question. My father was criticizing P.B. not for being a guru, but for not being the *right* guru. He was still searching. This May 1992 is his eightieth birthday. He is still searching.

Epilogue

What about my father, that other subject in the title of this book? After all, it was my father who exposed me to P.B., who encouraged me to see him the way he saw him, as the guru, the master, the sage. Although I have had many talks with him over the last year about P.B., I am still not certain who he thinks P.B. was. Unlike me, my father does not now feel betrayed; he has no sense of having wasted years of his life, no indignation. There is no disillusion for my father. When I gave him the sixteen volumes of P.B.'s posthumously published *Notebooks* to read, I thought that some of the obvious nonsense P.B. writes there would jolt him awake, would shake some of his reverence for P.B. I was wrong. "I described P.B. to you as a mystic," he told me when he finished, "but I made a mistake. In fact, he was truly a sage."

I don't think my father ever gave much thought to the risks he was taking in handing me over, spiritually speaking, to P.B. when I was still a small child. Since initially he believed everything P.B. told him, he of course saw me as privileged, not deprived or disadvantaged. It was my good karma that put me in touch with this luminary, this rishi, this mahatma, not bad fortune. In order to have been skeptical about my spending years in the company of P.B., he would have had to have been skeptical about P.B. himself. That was beyond my father's intellectual means. I cannot really blame him (or my mother, who was following my father, as she had been taught to do). They did the best they knew.

Bernard, my father, me—all of us—considered ourselves blessed to be involved, even on the periphery, of such extraordinary events as those we thought revolved around P.B. To be at the center of such cataclysmic changes was to be exalted. The world was changing, P.B. was about to take charge, and we were there, as his first lieutenants. To be part of this was a temptation that could not be resisted. To reject this opportunity, we would have had to have been mad, or to have thought that P.B. was mad. For a long time, such thoughts could not even be countenanced.

I cannot be as benignly resigned as my father ("it was fate"). But now, at fifty-one, I can look back upon the years spent with P.B. with some degree of nostalgia, even melancholy. The world was never again to seem so charged, so filled with mystery. P.B. dominated my childhood imagination with a seemingly never-ending supply of magic fantasies, higher powers, adverse forces, other planets, adepts in remote caves high in the Tibetan mountains, occult abilities, Egyptian magicians, Indian sages, astral travel, memories of ancient incarnations. I wish it were all true. I wish P.B. had been the person we all thought he was. How enchanting it would be to live with such a man, to be part of some master plan for the universe, the author of which shared one's bathroom. What a marvelous world to inhabit. Everything thereafter seemed drab by comparison. How could Harvard compete with Astral University? How could a train ride through France compete with heavenly journeys to distant galaxies? How could a struggling assistant professor compare with the ancient masters who taught at hidden universities fast in the Himalayas?

P.B.'s love of animals, his hatred of vivisection, his delight in the physical world around him struck a responsive chord in me as a child and still reverberate now. His love of nature affected me deeply. He had certain sensitivities that were highly developed, even if he thought they were highly evolved. Ever since I was a small child, he loved to take long walks with me, and I learned the pleasure to be found in an evening stroll. His favorite time of the day was sunset because, he often told us, it gives a hint of life's tragically passing character. He said that it touched his mind with melancholy to think that all of this beauty, which was so intense at that moment, was doomed to vanish very soon. Once when the sun was just about to set, he told me to see how the birds were all heading for their nests, and then he looked at me very intensely and said: "Jeff, this is your chance." I was not sure I understood, but I felt moved because I sensed that he wanted to provide me with what he had always called "the glimpse of the infinite." It was not enough for him simply to enjoy the beauty of it. Nevertheless, he did enjoy it, and so did I, and I enjoyed it often in his company. At those moments P.B. felt like a close friend, something I always wanted.

To some extent, what P.B. offered is offered by every guru. The implicit promises he made are made by all gurus, spiritual, psychoanalytic, or otherwise. P.B. offered wisdom, not knowledge; divine love, not human regard; visions, not insight; access to secret forces, not mediation; magic powers, not persuasion; mystery, secrecy, obfuscation, and paranoia. Every guru claims to know something you cannot know by yourself or through ordinary channels. All gurus promise access to a hidden reality if only you will follow their teaching, accept their authority, hand your life over to them. Every guru offers to read your past, or your future, or a past birth, or your hidden thoughts—and promises that you will develop the same ability. But you must always subordinate yourself to the guru. Certain questions are off limits. There are things you cannot know about the guru and the guru's personal life. To ask is at best impolite, at worst apostasy. Every doubt about the guru is a reflection of your own unworthiness, or the influence of an external evil force. You are not just expected to accept irrationality, you are to revel in it. The more obscure the action of the guru, the more likely it is to be right, to be cherished. Ultimately, you cannot admire the guru, you must worship him. You must obey him, you must humble yourself; for the greater he is, the less you are—until you too reach the inner circle and can start abusing other people the way your guru abused you. All of this is in the very nature of being a guru.

Every guru inflicts tyranny upon his disciples, every guru exploits his chelas, every guru dominates the student. Abuse is part of the definition, whether it is financial, emotional, sexual, physical, or intellectual. Once in, there is no escape. The best way out is never to go in.

To see deep into the structure of one tyranny is to understand something basic about all forms of oppression. It is totalitarian. Like other authoritarian systems, it requires a suspension and suppression of critical questioning; it demands unquestioning submission to a rigid hierarchical structure; it centers on a cult of personality, and it engenders personal intrusion and abuse.

As for P.B., I can't find it in my heart to hate him, or even to despise him. I am still left with the mystery of a human being who is more than the sum of his ignorance and his pretense. P.B. was less then he thought, but also more. He knew little, but he had a zest for life that was contagious and worth emulating. It was exciting to be in his presence, and it would have been just as exciting without all the hocus pocus and mumbo-jumbo, though he probably felt he could make no mark in the world without it. He brought solace and joy to many by making claims that were not true. I can fault him. I cannot forget him.